DATE DUE

Kate Chopin

Twayne's United States Authors Series

David J. Nordloh, Editor

Indiana University, Bloomington

TUSAS 485

KATE CHOPIN, 1899
Photograph courtesy of Missouri Historical Society, St. Louis

Kate Chopin

By Peggy Skaggs

Angelo State University

TWAYNE PUBLISHERS
An Imprint of Simon & Schuster Macmillan
NEW YORK

Prentice Hall International
LONDON · MEXICO CITY · NEW DELHI · SINGAPORE · SYDNEY · TORONTO

Kate Chopin

Peggy Skaggs

Copyright © 1985 by G. K. Hall & Company
All Rights Reserved
Published by Twayne Publishers
An Imprint of Simon & Schuster Macmillan
1633 Broadway
New York, NY 10019-6785

Book production by Beth Todesco

Book design by Barbara Anderson

Printed on permanent/durable acid-free
paper and bound in the United States of
America.

Library of Congress Cataloging in Publication Data

Skaggs, Peggy.
  Kate Chopin.

  (Twayne's United States authors series; TUSAS 485)
  Bibliography: p. 123
  Includes index.
  1. Chopin, Kate, 1851–1904—Criticism and interpretation.
I. Title. II. Series.
PS1294.C63S55   1985   813'.4   84-27977
ISBN 0-8057-7439-4

R5/00 Yale Research 32,00

To Merton

Contents

About the Author
Preface
Acknowledgments
Chronology

Chapter One
To the Beginning   1

Chapter Two
Critical Reputation   5

Chapter Three
Bayou Folk   12

Chapter Four
A Night in Acadie   27

Chapter Five
"A Vocation and a Voice"   39

Chapter Six
Miscellaneous Works   54

Chapter Seven
At Fault   73

Chapter Eight
The Awakening   88

Chapter Nine
Conclusions   112

Notes and References   115
Selected Bibliography   123
Index   129

About the Author

Peggy Skaggs, professor of English at Angelo State University in San Angelo, Texas, earned a B.A. from Southern Methodist University and M.A. and Ph.D. degrees from Texas A & M University. She has published articles on topics related to technical writing, pedagogy, folklore, and American literature in several journals, including *Technical Writing Teacher, Round Table, English in Texas, Southern Studies, American Literary Realism, 1890–1910*, and *American Literature.*

Preface

Many readers know Kate Chopin only as a writer of interesting, innocuous local-color short stories; many others, ironically, know her only through her daring novel *The Awakening*. Yet a study of her writing reveals a clear relationship between the "two Chopins," as well as a rapidly developed artistry.

That Chopin produced such a body of work in scarcely more than a decade surprises readers. But understanding how swiftly her ideas and her craftsmanship developed may surprise them even more. This book examines a few of Chopin's poems, all of her essays in literary criticism, and all of her fiction, tracing her remarkable literary progress from her first story, "Wiser than a God," to her last, "The Impossible Miss Meadows."

Complex, lifelike characters fill Chopin's stories. Vibrant personalities—young and old; white and black; male and female; Creole, "'Cadian," and "American"—people the pages of her fiction with all the diversity one finds in real life. But despite their differences, Chopin's characters often share one central quality: they seem to lack a clear concept of their own roles and purposes in life, a constant groping for such self-knowledge shaping their personalities and actions. As Chopin's artistry develops, this theme of the search for identity grows more insistent, reaching its apex in *The Awakening,* when Edna Pontellier decides to die rather than to live as less than a complete person.

To trace the progress of Chopin's literary art, then, requires a parallel consideration of the development of the search for identity as a theme in her fiction. This book relates the characters in the inoffensive local-color stories to the daring Edna Pontellier of *The Awakening* by following Chopin's concern with human identity throughout her career.

The first chapter briefly summarizes Chopin's life, emphasizing those aspects most closely related to her literature. Chapter 2 surveys the criticism and relates Chopin's fiction to the main currents in intellectual and literary tradition. Chapter 3 analyzes the short stories collected in her first volume, *Bayou Folk,* and chapter 4 those in her second volume, *A Night in Acadie.* Chapter 5 examines the stories in the projected but never published volume "A Vocation and a Voice." Chapter 6 analyzes the uncollected short stories, poems, and essays; chapter 7, the early novel *At Fault;* and chapter 8, her masterpiece, *The Awakening.* Finally, chapter 9 presents some conclusions based upon the analyses of the works.

Peggy Skaggs

Angelo State University

Acknowledgments

To the members of my family—my husband, Merton; my daughter, Angela; and my son, Mel—I wish to express my appreciation for making this book possible.

To Professor Katherine Bridges, Mrs. K. D. McCoy, and Archivist Beverly D. Bishop, I also wish to express my appreciation for their courtesy and help in locating and using materials at Northwestern State University in Natchitoches, Louisiana; at Bayou Folk Museum in Cloutierville, Louisiana; and at the Missouri Historical Society in St. Louis, Missouri.

To the members of my graduate committee in the English department at Texas A & M University—Professors Harrison E. Hierth, Richard H. Ballinger, and Carroll D. Laverty—I am also indebted for directing my first study of Kate Chopin, from which many of the ideas in this book evolved.

Further, I am indebted to Duke University Press, the Southern Studies Institute, and Louisiana State University Press for permission to quote from the folowing materials: (1) Peggy Skaggs, "The Boy's Quest in Kate Chopin's 'A Vocation and a Voice,'" *American Literature* 51 (1979):270–76, © 1979, Duke University Press; (2) Peggy Skaggs, "'The Man-Instinct of Possession': A Persistent Theme in Kate Chopin's Stories," *Southern Studies: An Interdisciplinary Journal of the South* (formerly *Louisiana Studies*) 14 (1975):277–85; (3) Peggy Skaggs, "Three Tragic Figures in Kate Chopin's *The Awakening*," *Southern Studies: An Interdisciplinary Journal of the South* (formerly *Louisiana Studies*) 13 (1974):345–64; and (4) Kate Chopin, *The Complete Works of Kate Chopin,* edited by Per Seyersted, © 1969, Louisiana State University Press.

Finally, I wish to acknowledge my gratitude to the Missouri Historical Society, St. Louis, for permission to use the photograph of Kate Chopin.

Chronology

1850   Catherine O'Flaherty (later Kate Chopin) born 12 July in St. Louis, Missouri.

1855   Thomas O'Flaherty, father of Catherine, dies.

1868   Graduates from the St. Louis Academy of the Sacred Heart.

1870   9 June, marries Oscar Chopin in St. Louis; the couple honeymoon in Europe until September; October, they move to New Orleans.

1871   Jean Chopin, Kate and Oscar's first son, born on 22 May in New Orleans.

1873   Oscar, Jr. (second son), born in St. Louis.

1874   George (third son), born in St. Louis.

1876   Frederick (fourth son), born in St. Louis.

1878   Felix (fifth son), born in New Orleans.

1879   Lelia (only daughter), born in New Orleans. Oscar's business fails. Family moves to Cloutierville, Louisiana.

1882   December, Oscar dies.

1884   Kate moves her family to St. Louis.

1885   June, Eliza O'Flaherty, Kate's mother, dies.

1889   27 October, first published story, "A Point at Issue," appears in *St. Louis Post-Dispatch.*

1890   September, *At Fault,* Chopin's first novel, published at her expense.

1890   Writes her second novel, "Young Dr. Gosse," between 4 May and 27 November; later destroys it.

1894   March, *Bayou Folk,* first volume of collected short stories.

1897   November, *A Night in Acadie,* second volume of collected stories.

1898   18 or 19 July, writes "The Storm."

1899   22 April, *The Awakening;* storm of critical and personal abuse follows.

1904   22 August, dies in St. Louis.

Chapter One
To the Beginning

Writing in the 1890s, Kate Chopin created hundreds of vibrant characters, most of whom are trying to satisfy three basic but often conflicting human drives that Chopin believes go together to make up a person's identity— the drives for a feeling of belonging, for love, and for a sense of individual sovereignty.

In every age the greatest writers have portrayed protagonists searching for a satisfactory sense of self. Christopher Marlowe's Faustus, for example, studies all fields of knowledge and turns at last to black magic when he realizes that he remains "but Faustus, and a man";[1] Shakespeare's Lear searches throughout the kingdom for an answer to his overwhelming question, "Who am I?"[2] And Chopin's characters approach life similarly, trying to discover who they are in this deepest sense of the term.

Perhaps because circumstances in her own life forced her repeatedly to adjust to the loss of a central figure, Chopin seems to have believed that our ideas of ourselves derive largely from our relationships with others, and that problems result when we compromise the need to establish ourselves as autonomous individuals in order to fulfill our needs to belong and to have satisfying relationships with others.

Kate O'Flaherty, the Child

The person who eventually became Kate Chopin first knew herself as Catherine O'Flaherty, born 12 July 1850, the daughter of Thomas and Eliza O'Flaherty. Born in Ireland in 1805, Thomas O'Flaherty had come to the United States in 1823. In 1825 he settled in St. Louis, where in time he grew prosperous as a merchant. In 1839 he married Catherine de Reilhe, a French-Creole girl, who died giving birth to their son, George; then in 1844 he married Eliza Faris, another French-American girl. Thomas and Eliza O'Flaherty produced three children: Jane, who died in childhood; Thomas, Jr., about whom we know little except that he was born in 1848 and died in 1873;[3] and Catherine, the youngest of the offspring and the one we know as Kate Chopin.

So Kate O'Flaherty first knew herself as Eliza and Thomas O'Flaherty's little girl. But in 1855 her father died suddenly, and his death thrust all his family into new relationships with each other and with the world; already, though barely five years old, Kate had to reshape her concept of herself. Not only was she abruptly stripped of the important relationship with her father; she was also forced into a new position with her mother, who of course was herself forced into a new role as a widow.

After her father's death Kate's family included the widowed mother, "a woman of great beauty, intelligence, and personal magnetism";[4] a widowed grandmother; and a widowed great-grandmother. The child's personal community also included her half-brother, George O'Flaherty, with whom she was emotionally close until his death in 1862, shortly after his release from a Union prison; her brother, Thomas; and assorted other relatives. Census records show that the O'Flaherty household abounded with people, usually including ten and never fewer than eight, during Kate's childhood and adolescence.[5]

Thus a number of close personal relationships marked Kate O'Flaherty's developing years, but death abruptly terminated several of these even before she entered her teens. Further, the early deaths of her father, grandfather, and great-grandfather prevented her as she matured from experiencing in her own family the traditional submissiveness of women to men.

The Debutante

In June 1868 Kate graduated from the St. Louis Academy of the Sacred Heart. She then "plunged into fashionable life, and for two years she was . . . 'one of the acknowledged belles of St. Louis.'"[6] Thus she found herself thrust into another new role, adjusting again to new relationships with people and to a new image of herself.

Kate O'Flaherty's entrance into St. Louis society signaled her readiness for wifehood, the role that has traditionally satisfied a woman's need for love and for a feeling of belonging. But the girl's rearing in a houseful of women and her education by nuns in a school for girls may not have prepared her to accept completely the limitations on a woman's autonomy that have traditionally accompanied wifehood. True, she must have been taught that she should become a traditional wife and mother, subordinating herself to masculine authority. But at both home and school she had, with few exceptions, seen only women actually exercising authority. Perhaps this inconsistency between training and experience contributed to the paradox between her own apparently happy marriage and her creation in fiction of female characters who feel stifled by the marriage relationship.

The Wife and Mother

In June 1870 Kate married Oscar Chopin of New Orleans, and she could hardly have had time to adjust to her new name and the role of wife to Oscar before taking on the still newer role of mother to her first son, Jean, who arrived on 22 May 1871. During the rest of the 1870s she fulfilled heavy social responsibilities as the wife of a prominent young Creole cotton broker, and she bore five more children in rapid succession. By 1879, then, when financial problems forced Oscar to move his family to Cloutierville, Louisiana, his wife probably retained little of Kate O'Flaherty, the St. Louis belle, in her mental image of herself.

The Widow

Oscar's sudden death in December 1882,[7] nevertheless, thrust Kate into yet another new role, forcing her to become widow and businesswoman. Then in 1884, after getting her Louisiana business affairs arranged, she moved with her children back to St. Louis to be near her mother and to resume in some sense the day-to-day role of daughter—only to have this relationship also abruptly terminated the next year by her mother's sudden death.

Thus Kate O'Flaherty Chopin's sense of who she was must have been constantly shifting to adjust to the loss of family members and to her changing place in her personal community. Small wonder, then, that many of her protagonists seem to be searching for self-understanding. Insofar as people know themselves through their relationships with others, Chopin's self-knowledge came largely from her relationships with a dimly remembered father; a dearly loved mother and great-grandmother; an unusually understanding, respected, and well-loved husband; and her six treasured, maturing children.

The Writer

In 1889 Chopin began writing fiction seriously. No one knows exactly why she took up her pen, but several influences probably contributed. First, she had always been a voracious reader; second, she needed to provide for her large family; third, her many friends with literary interests, especially Dr. Frederick Kolbenheyer,[8] encouraged her; and, finally, she had through almost thirty-nine years of living learned some things she wanted to say.

At any rate, in June 1889 she wrote her first story, "Wiser than a God," and by the end of 1889 she had written three other short stories and made good progress on *At Fault,* a promising novel which she published in 1890 at her own expense.[9] From that time her career progressed rapidly in both volume and quality until 22 April 1899, when the publisher Herbert S. Stone released *The Awakening.* But then the harsh critical reception given to this fine novel abruptly terminated Chopin's creative decade. Her death from a brain hemorrhage on 22 August 1904 seems almost anticlimactic beside the tragic extinction five years earlier of her creative life.

Although Per Seyersted has dated almost every story, and although every word Chopin is known to have written has now been published,[10] little evidence exists to connect particular stories with specific events in Chopin's life. In fact, although the basic events of her life are well established, little really is known about her personal life during the decade when she was writing.

Certainly her friend Dr. Kolbenheyer influenced her significantly. Apparently she was active in cultural organizations and maintained something of a salon during the 1890s;[11] yet the St. Louis Fine Arts Club ostracized her after the publication of *The Awakening.* All evidence collected by biographers Daniel S. Rankin and Per Seyersted suggests that Chopin's marriage was unusually fulfilling, that her husband in no way resembled the possessive husbands in her fiction, that she loved her children deeply, and that she usually wrote sitting in an armchair in a room filled with her children and their friends.[12]

Since Chopin was thirty-nine years old before she published her first story, she had already assimilated most of her formative experiences. Her unusual degree of personal maturity before beginning to write may explain the speed with which she found her central focus. Few writers have moved so far so rapidly as Chopin did between writing *At Fault* in 1889–90 and *The Awakening* in 1897–98.

Chapter Two
Critical Reputation

Irony has always marked Chopin's literary reputation, even as it marks much of her fiction. Her contemporaries praised warmly her early, often inferior, stories, especially those collected in *Bayou Folk* (1894) and to a lesser degree those in *A Night in Acadie* (1897).[1] But their bitter denunciation of her fine second novel, *The Awakening* (1899),[2] terminated her creative period and virtually banished her best work from critical consideration for half a century.

Chopin received only scattered attention during the first three decades of the century, but Dorothy Anne Dondore praised her in 1930 in the *Dictionary of American Biography,* saying that she "unveiled the tumults of a woman's soul" and that her having written *The Awakening* twenty years before its time was tragic. In 1932 Daniel S. Rankin published *Kate Chopin and her Creole Stories,* the first book-length work on Chopin. Today's scholar must thank Rankin for having collected most of the information known about her life and for having published eleven previously uncollected short stories. But Rankin, a Roman Catholic priest, had neither the background nor the mind-set to understand Chopin's main theme; and so he too ironically praises the weaker stories and condemns the stronger ones. Rankin even declares that Edna's statement in *The Awakening* that she would die for her children but would not give up "anything essential" for them was meaningless, although it "sounded clever because it was paradoxical."[3]

Rankin's work sparked little interest, and more than twenty years passed before the next important event in Chopin scholarship occurred. In 1953 a French scholar, Cyrille Arnavon, wrote a perceptive and influential essay to introduce his translation into French of *The Awakening.*[4] A few other critics of the 1950s, including especially Van Wyck Brooks[5] and Robert Cantwell,[6] express in brief comments admiration for Chopin's work. Robert Burton Bush devotes a chapter to Chopin in his 1957 doctoral dissertation, "Louisiana Prose Fiction: 1870–1900," noting that "Love is the great common denominator for almost all of the stories."[7] Master's theses by Merle Mae T. Jordan and Linda Wolfe round out the decade, with Jordan viewing Chopin as a social critic[8] and Wolfe commenting that the "essence" of *The Awakening* is Edna's discovery of both sensuality and selfhood.[9]

During the 1960s interest in Chopin increased markedly and began to focus on *The Awakening*, the novel's eroticism being overemphasized almost as much by critics of this decade as it had been by Chopin's contemporaries. Edmund Wilson says that Edna is simply a sensuous woman who follows her inclinations without thinking much about such issues as "free love or women's rights or the injustice of marriage."[10] Kenneth Eble follows Wilson in seeing Edna's problem simply as "a struggle with eros itself."[11]

But Carlos Baker believes that many of Chopin's best stories "turn upon acts of rebellion."[12] Warner Berthoff calls *The Awakening* "a New Orleans version of the familiar transcendentalist fable of the soul's emergence, or 'lapse,' into life," and believes Chopin's short stories are "less successful, relying excessively on Maupassantesque twists of ironic revelation on the last page."[13] Marie Fletcher says that rebellion leads Edna into experiences that thoroughly "awaken" her but that she cannot enjoy her "awakened" existence because "love . . . is also a threat to selfhood, which she still cannot surrender."[14] George Arms comments on Chopin's use of contrasts and her relativistic view of "truth."[15]

Lewis Leary, in one of the rare comments critics have made about *At Fault*, regards the earlier novel as a rough first design of "what later would be fashioned to art" in *The Awakening*.[16] And in an introduction to *The Awakening and Other Stories by Kate Chopin*, Leary finds Edna "a valiant woman, worthy of place beside other fictional heroines who have tested emancipation and failed—Nathaniel Hawthorne's Hester Prynne, Gustave Flaubert's Emma Bovary, or Henry James's Isabel Archer."[17]

Joan Zlotnick, in a brief article entitled "A Woman's Will: Kate Chopin on Selfhood, Wifehood, and Motherhood," asserts that Chopin's fiction is "a call to self-discovery"[18] and that her heroines often engage in a "desperate quest for freedom."[19] Larzer Ziff says that in *The Awakening* Chopin raises the question of how Edna's "life is related to the dynamics of her inner self." Yet incredibly Ziff, writing in 1966, can find "no sound reason" for Edna to feel stifled by her marriage.[20]

Certainly the most important events in Chopin studies occurred in 1969, when Per Seyersted wrote *Kate Chopin: A Critical Biography* and edited *The Complete Works of Kate Chopin*. His biography contains little new biographical information, but Seyersted interprets both Chopin's fiction and her life from a more modern perspective than had Rankin, commenting that in much of her work Chopin "was keeping up a running dialogue with herself on woman's lot."[21]

Seyersted's editorial work having made the body of Chopin's works conveniently available for the first time, many scholars in the 1970s focused less on familiarizing readers with her themes, merits, and shortcomings, and more on defining her place in the literary tradition. Even so, however, the irony that has always marked Chopin criticism continued, with critics during that decade describing her as a feminist, a local colorist, a regionalist, a romantic, a neotranscendentalist, an antiromantic, a realist, a naturalist, and an existentialist.

A number of critics have compared or contrasted Chopin's work with that of other individual writers. Pamela Gaudé in "Kate Chopin's 'The Storm': A Study of Maupassant's Influence"[22] studies that French writer's influence, to which Chopin herself attests in her essay "Confidences" (700–/01). Lisa Gerrard compares *Madame Bovary, La Regenta, The Mill on the Floss,* and *The Awakening.*[23] Whitman's influence is noted by Elizabeth B. House in *"The Awakening:* Chopin's 'Endlessly Rocking' Cycle,"[24] by Lewis Leary in "Kate Chopin and Walt Whitman,"[25] and by Gregory L. Candela in "Walt Whitman and Kate Chopin: A Further Connection."[26] Bernard J. Koloski identifies two lines of Swinburne's poetry near the end of *The Awakening,* which let the perceptive reader know of Edna's approaching suicide.[27] Gladys W. Milliner finds parallels between Chopin and Sylvia Plath in "The Tragic Imperative: *The Awakening* and *The Bell Jar.*"[28] In "The Limits of Passion," Sharon O'Brien discusses Willa Cather's 1899 review of *The Awakening.*[29] Susan Wolstenholme in "Kate Chopin's Sources for 'Mrs. Mobry's Reason'"[30] and William P. Warnken in "Kate Chopin and Henrik Ibsen: A Study of *The Awakening* and *A Doll's House"*[31] both note the influence of the Norwegian dramatist, whom Chopin herself describes as too concerned with social issues to achieve permanent significance (693).

Feminist critics have embraced Chopin enthusiastically. Joyce Ruddel Ladenson describes *The Awakening* as "a powerful story of one woman's education as antagonist against Victorian marriage and the social and psychological straightjacket it could produce."[32] In the spring of 1975 Emily Toth founded the *Kate Chopin Newletter,* which she continued to edit and publish through six issues in two volumes, until the spring 1977 issue, when she changed the journal's name to *Regionalism and the Female Imagination.* Toth says that in *The Awakening* Chopin translates into fiction the feminist arguments of Mary Wollstonecraft, Margaret Fuller, John Stuart Mill, August Bebel, and Charlotte Perkins Gilman against the economic, physical, and psychological confinement of women.[33] Toth has written several articles about Chopin, as well as editing the *Newletter* and assisting Per Seyersted in editing the *Kate Chopin Miscellany,* a collection that includes every previously unpublished word that Chopin is known to have written. In "The Independent Woman and 'Free' Love," Toth sees similarities among Chopin, George Sand, and Alexandra Kollontai, as all three writers confront the conflict between woman's desire for independence and traditional sexual restraints.[34] Feminist criticism has, in fact, been so effusive during the last decade that it has sometimes seemed to be turning Chopin's greatest literary art into a political tract. S. K. Oberbeck, writing in *Newsweek,* even goes so far as to attribute Chopin's "revival" more to her "oracular feminism and prophetic psychology" than to her literary talents.[35]

For many years most scholars knew Chopin only as a local colorist through a few often-anthologized stories, such as "The Bênitou's Slave" and "Désirée's Baby," and a few critics still emphasize her links with that nineteenth-century genre—for example, Sharon O'Brien in her 1976 article "Sentiment, Local Color, and the New Woman Writer: Kate Chopin and Willa Cather."[36] Jules Chametsky, in an essay treating George Washington Cable, Abraham Cahan, Charles W. Chestnut, and Kate Chopin, states that the stature of all four has been unfairly diminished because they have been designated "local color writers."[37] Some contemporary critics, however, seem more inclined to align Chopin with the romantics who preceded the local-color movement. Ottavio Mark Casale, for instance, relates Chopin's Edna to Hawthorne's Hester Prynne and to Melville's "composite figure of Ahab-Bulkington-Ishmael."[38] Elmo Howell says that "the end of her writing is to dramatize [the] conflict of body and soul."[39]

Also among critics who view Chopin's work as romantic is Donald A. Ringe, who reads *The Awakening* in terms of the transcendental concept of the soul's emergence into a new life, thus linking Chopin with Emerson and Whitman.[40] Charles W. Mayer in "Isabel Archer, Edna Pontellier, and the Romantic Self" contrasts Edna with Isabel, saying that both are married to insensitive, possessive men, but that their fates are due also to their own "egotism, willfulness, and perverseness." Mayer finds Edna unable to control her temperament and believes Isabel the more responsible.[41] Anne Goodwyn Jones studies the work of Chopin and six other women writers from Southern, upper-middle-class backgrounds. Jones argues that all seven are loyal to their region and its values but that their works challenge in various ways the notion that women must continue to nourish the genteel tradition.[42] House in "*The Awakening:* Kate Chopin's 'Endlessly Rocking' Cycle" declares that by consciously echoing Whitman's images and ideas, Chopin indicates that "Edna's suicide is affirmative, a beginning as well as an ending."[43]

On the other hand, several critics have viewed Chopin as antiromantic. For example, Gerrard believes that Edna's problems in *The Awakening* stem from an inherent conflict between her romanticism and an unromantic world. In "The Novel of Awakening" Susan J. Rosowski finds a common theme of "awakening to limitations" in *Madame Bovary, The Awakening, My Mortal Enemy, Daughter of Earth,* and *Middlemarch.*[44] Seeing Chopin as more radically antiromantic than do Gerrard and Rosowski, Otis B. Wheeler declares that, in spite of the Whitmanesque imagery, Edna's story rejects the "Romantic dream of the unlimited outward expansion of the self."[45]

Lewis P. Simpson, although finding romantic elements and pointing to parallels between Harriet Beecher Stowe and Chopin, says that Chopin (unlike Stowe) "explicitly grasped the nature and consequences of the worship of home and fireside." Simpson aligns Chopin with Poe, Melville, Hawthorne, Emerson, Thoreau, and Whitman in sharing a consciousness "of the vacuous condition following upon the loss of a transcendent meaning for human existence." Simpson notes also that, notwithstanding the psychological realism of George Washington Cable and Mark Twain, Chopin is the first writer to focus on the "sexual identity of the family and the individual in Southern settings." Further, Simpson says that, except for Whitman and Dreiser in their different ways, Chopin is the first American writer "to achieve a focus on the vexing and often agonizing relationship between sexual and social identity in American society." Simpson believes that Mark Twain by writing *The Mysterious Stranger* tried to bring under the control of art his despair over the destruction of the moral interpretation of the world, and that Chopin wrote *The Awakening* under the same impulse. Because Twain, except through the persona of Huck Finn, never achieved the detachment of the modern literary artist, he left *Stranger* unfinished; but Chopin did successfully achieve such a perspective. Simpson says that Edna, like Huck Finn, is "a self-creating character, one who . . . has a life larger than the confines of the story." Thus Simpson concludes that Chopin made a significant contribution to late nineteenth-century realism.[46]

Sarah Patricia H. Lattin agrees with Simpson that Chopin's "method" is that of the realistic movement, but declares that her "vision" is not. This critic asserts that Chopin's "solution to the romantic alienation of the individual and her understanding of the process of achieving selfhood often reflect a late-nineteenth-century form of transcendentalism."[47]

Several critics compare and contrast Chopin and Dreiser, with a few even identifying Chopin as a thorough-going naturalist. Toth, in "Timely

and Timeless: The Treatment of Time in *The Awakening* and *Sister Carrie,*"
finds fundamental differences that outweigh "superficial similarities in plot
and reception" between the two novels.[48] Seyersted says that Chopin concentrates on biological aspects of woman's situation while Dreiser, Norris,
Garland, and Crane all concentrate on socioeconomic forces shaping her
life.[49] Nancy Walker declares that Edna's awakening is altogether sensual
and depends largely upon the "Louisiana Creole setting and the naturalistic
literary convention" of Chopin's day.[50] Barbara Culver Van Sittert also sees
Chopin's fiction as naturalistic in "Social Institutions and Biological Determinism in the Fictional World of Kate Chopin."[51] Harry Scott Butler says
that Chopin sometimes treats human sexuality in the manner of a naturalist but that at other times she views it from a romantic-transcendental
perspective. This ambivalence, Butler believes, reflects Chopin's responsiveness to nineteenth-century intellectual currents.[52]

Jerome Klinkowitz in *The Practice of Fiction in America* brings together
the various perspectives on Chopin's place in the tradition; he observes,
"Chopin's development as a writer . . . reflects in microcosm the larger
movement in American literature from romanticism and local color to realism and naturalism. . . . Chopin's stories and novels reflect . . . clearly
the general trend in American literature of that era. Her theme is a romantic imaginative awakening; the catalyst for it is drawn from the materials
of local color; and her method of following the action is naturalistic."[53]
Thus the seemingly contradictory critical views of Chopin's fiction may not
be so contradictory after all.

As early as 1966 Stanley Kaufmann notes Chopin's prophetic existentialism in *The Awakening.*[54] In his *Critical Biography* Seyersted describes the
novel similarly. And in "Kate Chopin: Her Existential Imagination"
Eleanor B. Wymard explores this perspective thoroughly; she argues that
the thrust of existentialism has always been to establish the separate identity of the individual. Wymard describes Edna as needing "to know and
express her inner being." The novel's conflict, then, grows out of Edna's
coming to understand but not to accept the chains imposed on her by
"biology, convention, and social morality." Wymard points out that "Although words such as 'authentic self' and 'becoming' suggest jargon, Chopin used them in 1899 (*The Awakening*) to uncover the realities of modern
woman's predicament. . . . Personhood is indeed Chopin's theme."[55]

Chopin, in her essay "Confidences," admires Maupassant for having "escaped from tradition and authority" and for having "entered into himself
and looked out upon life through his own being and with his own eyes"
(701). The myriad views of Chopin's place in the American literary tradi-

tion attest to her having made a similar escape from tradition and authori-ty. Clearly, Flaubert and especially Maupassant influenced her. Certainly Hawthorne, Melville, Poe, Emerson, and most importantly Whitman helped to shape her responses to life. Undoubtedly, her works contain traces of the romantic, transcendental, local-color, realistic, and naturalistic movements. But Chopin transcends her sources and influences to create a body of work that speaks in its own voice. That voice prophesies the plea of the twentieth-century feminist and the lonely cry of the existentialist. But those later traditions can no more contain the voice than could the earlier ones. Chopin's voice remains her own, growing ever clearer and more insistent throughout her creative decade in declaring that unless one's inner person is integral with one's outer roles and relationships a fully satisfying life cannot be achieved.

Chapter Three
Bayou Folk

The critical praise Chopin received during her lifetime resulted largely from her short stories, most of which belong to the local-color tradition. *Bayou Folk* (1894), her first collection of short stories, contains twenty-three such tales, all but four having been published previously in popular journals.[1] The stories are set in Louisiana, most of them in Natchitoches Parish, and since many of the characters appear in more than one tale,[2] a loose unity develops. Most of the stories, somewhat superficial and sentimental, reveal their origin as popular magazine fiction. Yet even in these early stories Chopin's characters are struggling to find a place of their own in their communities; some are trying to cope with their need for love; and a few are already reaching timidly for autonomy, thus foreshadowing later strong characters, including Edna in *The Awakening*.

The *Bayou Folk* stories fall loosely into five groups: those that feature self-reliant young girls as protagonists; those that study the lingering dislocations caused by the Civil War; those that center upon emancipated black people who in seeking a place in society deny even their freedom; those that examine love between the sexes; and those that hint at the theme of male possessiveness. To some extent these concerns overlap, several stories treating more than one. And many of the stories address, at least obliquely, Lear's question—the question that lies at the heart of most of Chopin's later, more important fiction and that finally comes into clear focus in *The Awakening*—"Who am I?"

Self-Reliant Young Girls

Several of the stories portray exceptionally self-reliant young girls. In "A Rude Awakening," for example, Lolotte, barely seventeen years old, tries valiantly to care for three younger brothers but in doing so loses her identity and almost loses her life. Trying to substitute for her lazy father, old Sylveste, Lolotte attempts to drive a team and wagon to the landing. The team runs away, wrecking the wagon and leaving no trace of the girl. Guilt-ridden, Sylveste abandons his careless ways and takes a job with Joe

Duplan, a neighboring planter. Duplan finally finds Lolotte in a New Orleans hospital suffering from amnesia, a rather common disorder in Chopin's characters. Upon seeing the planter, the girl remembers who she is; and Duplan returns her to her father, admonishing him never to forget again "that you are a man!" (144). Here the story ends, with Lolotte, the self-reliant child, now having a role in caring for her brothers that is more appropriate to her age and strength, because her father has "awakened" to his responsibilities.

Similarly, in "A Gentleman of Bayou Têche" Martinette's father, Evariste, depends upon his young daughter. The two Acadians, so impoverished that even the Negroes look down upon them, are overjoyed because a man wants to hire Evariste to pose for a painting. But when old Aunt Dicey jealously tells Martinette that "Dey gwine sot down on'neaf the picture: 'Dis heah is one dem low-down 'Cajuns o' Bayeh Têche!'" (320), Martinette orders her father not to pose. So Evariste goes fishing instead, and thus happens to be at the bayou when the painter's son almost drowns. Of course, Evariste rescues the child, and the grateful father promises to label his picture "A hero of Bayou Têche." But Evariste does not consider himself a hero; finally, the painter tells Evariste to caption the picture himself, and the Acadian tells him to write "Dis is one picture of Mista Evariste Anatole Bonamour, a gent'man of de Bayou Têche" (324), showing that he has a healthy sense of his own dignity as a human being.

Not very different from Lolotte and Martinette, though even younger, a little barefooted girl named Fifine in "A Very Fine Fiddle" sells her father's violin, getting for it "a fiddle twice as beautiful . . . and a roll of money besides . . . enough to put shoes on all the little bare feet and food into the hungry mouths" (150). Equally pragmatic is Boulotte in "Boulôt and Boulotte," who at the age of twelve gets her first pair of shoes but carries them home in her hand so she will not "ruin it in de dus'" (152). "A Turkey Hunt" presents Artemise, a young black protagonist less easily understood than these Acadian girls. In fact, "Pages might be told of her unfathomable ways" (192). But she has one outstanding characteristic, a placid self-containment that suggests she feels quite complete within herself.

In "Loka" Chopin creates yet another young girl who accepts great responsibility. Loka, a teenage, half-Indian girl, does not know exactly what her place is or where she belongs: "she said her name was Loka, and she did not know where she belonged, unless it was on Bayou Choctaw" (212). She appears in Natchitoches from nowhere and is placed in the Padue home, where she will "not only be taught to work . . . but . . . receive a good moral training beside." Madame Tontine Padue begins the "training" by demanding to know why Loka does not know French. The youngster replies apologetically, "I kin talk English good's anybody; and lit' bit Choctaw, too." The girl's slowness provokes Tontine. Monsieur Padue reminds his wife that "She 's on'y a chile, rememba," but Tontine retorts, "She 's *vrai sauvage* that 's w'at. It 's got to be work out of her"(213). Thus Tontine attempts, unconsciously but furiously, to destroy Loka's identity both as a Choctaw and as a child.

Loka grows to love little Bibine, the baby. But one day when she finds herself left alone with the baby, homesickness washes over her: "Her heart was aching with savage homesickness. . . . She felt she must die if she could not get back to [the woods] and to her vagabond life. . . . She stooped and unlaced the brogans that were chafing her feet . . . and threw the things away from her. She stood up all a-quiver, panting, ready for flight" (215). But the sound of little Bibine's cooing stops her. She cannot leave him behind.

When the family returns, however, they find that both Loka and Bibine have disappeared. First furious and then pale and quiet, Tontine reacts "with an unnatural calm that frightened the children" (216). At dusk, the girl and the baby return, only to be met by Tontine's renewed fury and her threat to send Loka "back to that ban' w'ere you come from." Loka explains that she and the baby had "jis' go take lit' 'broad in de wood" (217) because she had felt unbearably homesick but could not leave the baby she loves. Her explanation, however, does not move Tontine.

Monsieur Padue asserts himself at this point, declaring that Tontine has been too harsh: "she done tole us how she was temp' to-day to turn *canaille*—like we all temp' sometime'. W'at was it save her? That li'le chile w'at you hole in yo' arm" (217–18). Thus Monsieur Padue recognizes that Loka has acted responsibly, placing her love for the infant ahead even of her own yearnings for freedom.

These young girls—Lolotte, Martinette, Fifine, Boulotte, Artemise, and Loka—demonstrate such self-sufficiency that one can scarcely imagine their growing up to be the helpless, self-effacing mothers and wives that society would push them to become. Serious conflicts must develop inside a person who must respond to such grossly contradictory expectations.

Lingering Dislocations

The stories that examine the lingering effects of the Civil War center on the theme of dislocation. The title character in "Old Aunt Peggy," for example, is a freed slave who, by her own choice, remains virtually unchanged by the war or emancipation, clinging to the place where she feels secure and giving up entirely any active role in life.

One of Chopin's several studies of mental disorder that resulted from the war, "Beyond the Bayou" features Jacqueline, who has refused to cross the bayou for thirty years because she had been frightened "out of her senses" (175) when P'tit Maître came wounded to her cabin during the war. But thirty years later, when P'tit Maître's son Chéri is accidentally wounded near Jacqueline's cabin, love gives her the courage to cross the bayou for help. As a result, "a look of wonder and deep content crept into her face as she watched for the first time the sun rise upon the new, the beautiful world beyond the bayou" (180). Love has great healing power in Chopin's fictive world.[3]

Ma'ame Pélagie, in a story of the same name, "adjusts" to the dislocations of the war much as Old Aunt Peggy and Jacqueline do. A fifty-year-old spinster with an air of queenly authority, Ma'ame lives with her sister, Pauline, near Valmêt, the family's mansion that the war had destroyed. They manage the plantation prosperously, working hard and saving every cent they make toward Ma'ame's one goal in life, restoring Valmêt. Their happiest moments occur on pleasant afternoons when they drink their black coffee on the portico of the old ruin, "with only each other and the sheeny, prying lizards for company, talking of the old times and planning for the new" (232–33). The "new" times they plan for, however, would be no newer than Aunt Peggy's.

Eventually the ladies' niece, La Petite, comes to live with them, bringing new life and love into their sterile world. But La Petite soon declares that she is going back to her father's home because living as her aunts do is for her "a sin against myself" (235). Love for La Petite proves stronger even than Ma'ame's need to restore her former place in the world; and so, sacrificing all her dreams, she decides to eradicate the old ruin and build a modern, new home.

Within a year, the faces of the sisters reveal the results. The younger sister seems revitalized: her "cheek was as full and almost as flushed as La Petite's. The years were falling away from her." But the older sister shows a different effect: "In her deep, dark eyes smouldered the light of fires that would never flame. She had grown very old" (238–39). Pauline, only five years old when the sisters had lost their way of life, needed only the opportunity to find a new place in the new world. But Ma'ame Pélagie, twenty when the holocaust came, had lost her home, her way of life, and also the man she loved. Such losses proved too great to overcome.

"A Wizard of Gettysburg" combines the war-dislocation theme with another case of Chopin's favorite mental illness, amnesia. Bertrand Delmandé takes mercy on a tramp, who coincidentally turns out to be his grandfather, a victim of amnesia, believed lost thirty years before in the war. The sight of the boy jolts the old man enough to make him remember having had a son and daughter, but he mistakes his grandchildren for the now-grown children and has no flicker of recognition for his now-old wife. Obviously, he still sees himself as a young man with young children and a young wife.

Monsieur Jean Baptiste Plochel in "The Return of Alcibiade" lives in delusion, awaiting the return of his son, Alcibiade, who died in the war. The son had promised to return for Christmas dinner, and one Christmas a young man happens to have buggy trouble near Plochel's plantation. The old man cries, "À la fin! mon fils! à la fin!" (250). His granddaughter explains, convincing the young man to pretend to be Alcibiade, and everything works out well. The old man takes a nap after dinner, happy for the first time in thirty years; and he dies in his sleep, secure in his role of father.

Old Aunt Peggy, Jacqueline, Ma'ame Pélagie, Grandfather Delmandé, and Monsieur Plochel, then, have much in common because the war thirty years before had dislocated each in some fundamental way, leaving her or him unable to find a secure, productive place in the new order.

Emancipated Blacks

Many of these *Bayou Folk* stories, set in the South approximately thirty years after the Emancipation Proclamation, feature black people coping in various ways with the special identity problems that accompanied their freedom. For example, as noted above, Old Aunt Peggy simply withdraws from the struggle and waits to die. Others, as will be noted later, find happier places in society to replace the one lost through freedom.

Two stories, however, portray blacks who cope only by trying to hang onto their old identity as slave members of white families. In "For Marse Chouchoute" a young black protagonist named Wash suffers fatal injuries while doing a job that Chouchoute, a young white boy, should be doing. As he dies, Wash cries out, "I boun' to git well, 'ca'se who—gwine— watch Marse—Chouchoute?" (110).

In much the same way, "The Bênitou's Slave" also develops the theme that a person needs to feel that he or she belongs somewhere. Uncle Oswald, who had belonged to the Bênitou family fifty years before, spends his life trying to get back to his "own" family. At last an unlikely coincidence leads Uncle Oswald to meet the tiny remainder of his old family—a little milliner and her daughter. They agree to let Uncle Oswald stay with them, making him happy because now he feels that he belongs. He knows now who he is: "My name 's, Oswal', Madam; Oswal'—dat's my name. I b'longs to de Bênitous" (190).

Much as one may deplore the stereotyped "befo' de wa'" image of the black men[4] in these two stories, their actions do represent one direction sometimes taken in the search for an identity to replace one lost through emancipation. Chopin understands a basic need of the emancipated black man and the "emancipated" woman: both need deeply to find a new place in society. Both have for centuries been encouraged by white men to "know their place" and to "stay in their place." And both have encountered difficulty in finding a new place after becoming free. So the stories of these two self-effacing Negro characters illuminate later female creations by Chopin, notably the similar character of Adéle Ratignolle in *The Awakening,* the most nearly perfect of the "mother-women . . . who idolized their children, worshiped their husbands, and esteemed it a holy privilege to efface themselves as individuals. . . ." (888).

Love Between the Sexes

The remainder of the stories in *Bayou Folk* revolve around love between the sexes and the complex ways in which love affects one's feelings about oneself.

In "Love on the Bon-Dieu" Chopin again displays her interest in mental disorders. A young couple, Lalie and Azenor, become acquainted through a priest, Lalie's only contact with any person other than the mad grandmother with whom she lives. Lalie tries to explain her situation to Azenor: "Po' ole Grand'mère! . . . I don' b'lieve she know mos' time w'at she 's doin'. Sometime she say' I ain't no betta an' one nigga, an' she fo'ce me to work. Then she say she know I 'm goin' be one canaille like maman, an' she make me set down still, like she would want to kill me" (160). Yet despite her grandmother's irrational attacks on her sense of who she is, Lalie seems unusually self-confident, perhaps because her grandmother clearly needs her.

But when Lalie falls ill, Azenor decides that he must take her away. Although he has no idea of where to take her, he feels that "there must be one somewhere with the spirit of Christ" who will make a place for her. Lifting her in his arms, however,

> he saw that she held . . . the pretty Easter-egg he had given her! He uttered a low cry of exultation. . . .
> No need now to go . . . begging admittance for her. . . . He knew now where her place was. (162)

So, Lalie and Azenor in finding each other discover both place and love.

In "A No-Account Creole" the protagonist, Euphrasie, almost waits too long before discovering her right place in life. Placide Santien, with a possessive attitude much like that of Léonce Pontellier in *The Awakening* and of numerous other Creole gentlemen in Chopin's fiction, has regarded Euphrasie as his own ever since she was placed in his arms on his sixth birthday. Years later, asking her to marry him, he demands to know: "Do you love anybody better? . . . Any one jus' as well as me?" She replies honestly, "You know I love papa better, Placide, an' Maman Duplan jus' as well" (86). But knowing no reason to refuse to marry Placide, she accepts. Soon, however, Wallace Offdean[5] arrives, and Euphrasie discovers within herself strange, new feelings—almost another person— as she becomes better acquainted with Offdean.

One night Placide kisses her passionately on the lips. Afterwards, "She . . . sobbed a little and prayed a little. She felt that she had sinned, . . . a fine nature warned her that it was in Placide's kiss" (95). Placide, upon learning Euphrasie's feelings, frees her to marry Offdean, her true love.

Chopin comes close in this story to having her protagonist marry a man she does not love because of having committed herself before knowing her own heart. Later, in *The Awakening,* the writer will confront directly the problems involved in exactly such a marriage, that of Edna and Léonce Pontellier, whose marriage "was purely an accident." Léonce, like Placide, "fell in love . . . and pressed his suit." And Edna, like Euphrasie, feels affection but no passion, "realizing with some unaccountable satisfaction that no trace of passion . . . colored her affection" (898). In the later story, however, the couple have been married for several years and have produced two children before Edna makes her own discovery that parallels Euphrasie's, finding within herself strange new feelings, almost another person inside her old self.

Even in these earliest stories, Chopin almost always creates with great economy a unified effect. But "In and Out of Old Natchitoches" begins developing in one direction and then does an abrupt about-face. The author apparently creates a dilemma for her characters that she is either unwilling to confront or unable to resolve in her own mind. The first part of this story places the central character, Mademoiselle Suzanne St. Denys Godolph, in conflict with Alphonse Laballière. Suzanne, a school teacher of proud Creole stock, refuses to accept as a pupil a mulatto child whom Alphonse, of equally aristocratic old South blood, tries to force into her school, either simply to prove that he can do so or, perhaps, to express his disgust that such a high-born lady would actually lower herself so far as to accept paid employment.

To resolve this dramatic situation, Chopin simply changes focal points in mid-story. Suzanne moves to New Orleans, where she falls a bit in love with a distant cousin, Hector Santien. Alphonse follows, uncovers the cousin's secret identity as a notorious gambler, and saves the girl in spite of herself.

After exposing the cousin's vice-filled life, Alphonse returns to Natchitoches on the same train with Suzanne: "He went to her . . . and held out his hand; she extended her own unhesitatingly. She could not understand why. . . . It seemed as though the sheer force of his will would carry him to the goal of his wishes" (266). This scene echoes Euphrasie's earlier decision to marry Placide because "she saw no reason why she should not" (86), and it foreshadows Edna's later decision to marry Léonce when he "pressed his suit" (898).

A bit more daring, "In Sabine" focuses on 'Tite Reine, a miserable young wife whose husband mistreats her cruelly. Before her marriage, she had been a charming girl, with "her trim, rounded figure; her . . . saucy . . . coquettish eyes, her little . . . imperious ways . . . her . . . nickname of 'Tite Reine, little queen" (326). But that picture contrasts sadly with the girl Grégoire Santien finds when he visits her in Sabine Parish only a year after her marriage: "her eyes were larger, with an alert, uneasy look in them. . . . her shoes were in shreds." Worse, her "little imperious ways" have changed into a habitual response to her husband's call: "I 'm comin', Bud. Yere I come. W'at you want, Bud?" (327). Taking mercy on the poor girl, Grégoire plies Bud with whiskey so that 'Tite Reine may escape to the safety of her old home. Happy to see her escape, the reader does not wonder much about what sort of place she will find awaiting her as a "feme sole" back on Bayou Pierre.

"La Belle Zoraïde," a sad love story, centers upon a pampered slave girl, who certainly has a secure place but no love and no autonomy at all. Madame Delarivière has reared Zoraïde, the beautiful black protagonist, in her own image: "As charming and as dainty as the finest lady of la rue

Royale" (304), Zoraïde does no work that might roughen her hands. In
fact, she has her own little black servant. Madame often tells Zoraïde about
the wedding that will someday join her with M'sieur Ambroise, the body
servant of Doctor Langlé. But Zoraïde finally tells Madame that she loves
Mézor, a field hand. Madame exclaims, "That negro! that negro! . . . but
this is too much!" Zoraïde, nevertheless, pleads with simple logic: "Am I
white, nénaine? . . . Doctor Langlé gives me his slave to marry, but he
would not give me his son. Then, since I am not white, let me have from
out of my own race the one whom my heart has chosen" (305).

Of course, Madame forbids Zoraïde and Mézor to marry, but she cannot
prevent their loving, as the black woman narrating the story to her own
white mistress points out. Zoraïde becomes pregnant and breaks the news
to Madame, saying, "Kill me if you wish, nénaine: forgive me if you will;
but when I heard le beau Mézor say to me, 'Zoraïde, mo l'aime toi,' I could
have died, but I could not have helped loving him" (305).

At this point, Madame induces Dr. Langlé to sell Mézor. Then when
Zoraïde delivers her child, Madame takes the baby away and tells Zoraïde
that it was stillborn. Having thus disposed of Zoraïde's lover and baby,
Madame returns to her plan to marry the girl to Dr. Langlé's body servant,
and the slave girl seems to submit "as though nothing mattered any longer
in this world" (306–7). But Zoraïde manages to elude her owner's plans
again.

Shortly before the scheduled wedding, the young woman begins carrying in her arms a "senseless bundle of rags shaped like an infant." All treat-
ments, even returning to her arms her own child, prove useless, and the
poor girl lives out her days imagining herself the mother of a pile of rags.
"She was never known again as la belle Zoraïde, but ever after as Zoraïde
la folle" (307). "La Belle Zoraïde" thus illustrates one of Chopin's best
themes: that tragedy results when a person is robbed of her right to be her
own person and to love whom she will.

Madame Delisle, the title character of "A Lady of Bayou St. John," like
Zoraïde finds her identity in an imaginary role. Madame's husband, Gustave, goes away to the war, leaving a beautiful but childish wife behind.
Sepincourt, a neighbor, and the lonely lady fall in love and decide to run
away together. But that very night Madame learns that her husband has
died. Sepincourt impatiently waits until he can without indecency again
speak of his love; but when he does go to her, she greets him "precisely as
she . . . welcomed the curé, . . . clasping his two hands warmly, and calling him 'cher ami.' Her whole attitude . . . brought the bewildering conviction that he held no place in her thoughts" (300). Nevertheless, he

declares: "I have come now . . . to ask you to be my wife, my companion, the dear treasure of my life" (301). But having discovered a new, satisfying role as a widow, a new place in life wherein she feels comfortable, she answers:

"can you not understand, *mon ami*, . . . that now such a thing . . . is impossible to me?"

"Impossible?"

"Yes, impossible. Can you not see that now . . . my very life, must belong to another? . . ."

"Would you . . . wed your young existence to the dead?" he exclaimed with . . . horror. . . .

"My husband has never been so living to me as he is now," she replied. (301)

The narrator emphasizes Madame's kinship with poor "Zoraïde la folle," as both women live out their lives wrapped in the mantle of an illusory identity: "Madame still lives on Bayou St. John. She is rather an old lady now. . . . The memory of Gustave still fills . . . her days" (302). Surely, Madame is also "la folle."

"Madame Célestin's Divorce" suggests the mysterious power of love and the tenacity with which a woman may cling to a place where she feels she belongs. Madame—who, significantly, has no name except her husband's—attracts the love of another man, Lawyer Paxton, while her husband is on one of his prolonged absences. Paxton encourages her to divorce Célestin—who drinks, lies, leaves home periodically, and neglects his family in every way. If she divorces Célestin, she will encounter the disapproval of family, community, and church; but she is prepared to "face it and brave it" (277). Lawyer Paxton plans to settle in a new location, where he and a new family can make a new start.

But one morning, looking "unusually rosy" and wearing a pink bow, Madame Célestin tells Paxton: "I reckon you betta neva mine about that divo'ce. . . . You see, Judge, Célestin came home las' night. An' he 's promise me on his word an' honor he 's going to turn ova a new leaf" (279). Thus, Madame's love for Célestin and perhaps her sense of belonging with him have preserved their marriage, such as it is, thereby accomplishing what the combined disapproval of family, community, and church could not.

Another story about marriage, "A Visit to Avoyelles," features a wife whose relationship with her husband and children seems to fill her emotional needs quite well. The protagonist, Mentine, has been married to

Jules Trodon for seven years, and to show for those years she has babies, "as good as four already" (228); ragged clothes; a voice grown shrill from screaming at the children; a misshapen but piteously thin figure; and skin like parchment. Doudouce, her suitor before Jules entered her life, still loves her and finds the gossip about her hard lot unbearable. Feeling that he must know the truth, he visits the Trodons' home, where the couple greet him warmly. Doudouce notes that seven years of marriage have not changed Jules except to make him "broader, stronger, handsomer" (230); but Jules's welfare contrasts sharply with Mentine's pitiful condition. Nevertheless Doudouce "loved her now as he never had. . . . because she was in a manner fallen; because she was Mentine, he loved her" (231).

Far from having "fallen" from her old existence, however, Mentine has in actuality been reborn into her new one, a fact that soon becomes apparent to Doudouce. The two men leave after lunch, walking away in different directions; and "after a moment or two Doudouce looked back at Mentine, standing at the gate with her baby. But her face was turned away from him. She was gazing after her husband who went in the direction of the field" (231). Thus, even amid her difficult circumstances, Mentine obviously feels that her marriage fulfills her needs for belonging and love, and she shows no longing to change anything about her life.

"The Man-Instinct of Possession"

"At the 'Cadian Ball" and "Désirée's Baby" treat related ideas that become increasingly important in Chopin's later works. The theme of masculine pride in "owning" a beautiful wife from the highest social stratum possible—what Chopin later calls "the man-instinct of possession" (401)—ties these two stories together and relates them to some of the writer's most mature works as well.[6]

In at least two important ways "At the 'Cadian Ball" foreshadows later Chopin works. First, it lays the groundwork for its sequel, "The Storm," an almost perfect short story written six years later and so startlingly frank that Chopin never even tried to have it published.[7] And second, the story introduces Alcée Laballière, a man in many ways like Léonce Pontellier in *The Awakening*. The two men share the qualities of kindness and decency as well as a French Creole heritage, social prominence, wealth, and pride in their aristocratic backgrounds. But most important, each man believes that the woman he marries should be, like the largest and brightest jewel ornamenting a monarch's crown, his most prized possession. Early in *The Awakening,* Léonce looks at his wife "as one looks at a valuable piece of personal property" (882), and a careful reader will sense that in "At the

'Cadian Ball" Alcée feels a similar possessiveness toward Clarisse, the girl he wants to marry.

"At the 'Cadian Ball" begins with a description of "big, brown, good-natured" Bobinôt, an Acadian farmer, who loves a Spanish girl named Calixta, described as he visualizes her: "Her eyes . . . the . . . most tantalizing that ever looked into a man's; . . . that broad, smiling mouth and tiptilted nose, that full figure; that voice like a rich contralto song . . . taught by Satan." Bobinôt thinks at first that he will not go to the ball, even though he knows that Calixta will be there, because "what came of those balls but heartache . . . ?" (219). When he hears that the handsome, young planter Alcée Laballière may attend, however, Bobinôt changes his mind. A breath of scandal had stirred the year before when Calixta and Alcée were both at Assumption, but no one talks of it now. Still, Bobinôt thinks of Alcée: "A drink or two could put the devil in his head . . . ; a gleam from Calixta's eyes, a flash of her ankle, a twirl of her skirts could do the same" (220). So Bobinôt decides to go to the ball after all.

Next the story introduces Alcée and Clarisse. Alcée, gambling heavily by having planted nine hundred acres of rice, will either make or lose a very great deal of money, and he works hard because of the high stakes and the dramatic challenge. Clarisse, his distant cousin and his mother's godchild, lives with the Laballière family. She is "dainty as a lily; . . . slim, tall, graceful. . . . Cold and kind and cruel by turn, and everything that was aggravating to Alcée." Clarisse's guests often fill the big plantation house. But Alcée "would have liked to sweep the place of those visitors, often. Of the men, above all, with . . . their swaying of fans like women, and dandling about hammocks. He could have pitched them over the levee into the river, if it had n't meant murder. That was Alcée." However, he treats Clarisse gently until one day when his passion overcomes him: "he came in from the rice-field, and, toil-stained as he was, clasped Clarisse by the arms and panted a volley of hot, blistering love-words into her face. No man had ever spoken love to her like that" (220). Clarisse, the true blue blood, handles the situation with haughty ease: "'Monsieur!' she exclaimed, looking him full in the eyes, without a quiver. Alcée's hands dropped and his glance wavered before the chill of her calm, clear eyes." But she continues: "'*Par exemple!*' she muttered disdainfully, as she turned from him, deftly adjusting the careful toilet that he had so brutally disarranged" (220–21).

A day or two later a storm destroys the rice crop. Although he maintains an icy silence, Alcée looks ill and gray. "Clarisse's heart melted with tenderness; but when she offered her soft, purring words of condolence, he accepted them with mute indifference" (221). One night soon, however,

Clarisse happens to see Alcée ride away sometime around midnight. She forces from his servant the information that Alcée is going to the 'Cadian ball to have a "li'le fling" that will take his mind off his troubles. Clarisse reacts with contempt.

Both of the two couples—Bobinôt and Calixta, Alcée and Clarisse— seem to belong together. In each instance, the two share similar social statuses, financial resources, goals in life, ideals, value systems, life-styles.

But in another sense, Alcée and Calixta belong together too. The young planter really goes to the ball to rekindle the fire that he and Calixta had merely banked at Assumption the preceding year. And as soon as they see each other, the passion flames anew. They stroll into the garden and exchange teasing, bantering words:

"There is Bobinôt looking for you. You are going to set poor Bobinôt crazy. You 'll marry him some day; *hein,* Calixta?"

"I don't say no, me," she replied, striving to withdraw her hand, which he held more firmly for the attempt. . . .

Calixta's senses were reeling; and they well-nigh left her when she felt Alcée's lips brush her ear. (224–25).

At this point, a servant interrupts to give Alcée a message from "some one in de road" who wants to see him. The gentleman declares that he would not go out to the road "to see the Angel Gabriel" (225) and threatens to break the black man's neck should another interruption occur.

But Clarisse herself interrupts Alcée and Calixta next, declaring that she "could n't stan' it" (227) if Alcée does not come home and adding, "Not to frighten you. But you mus' come" (225). Whereupon, "Alcée swung himself over the low rail and started to follow Clarisse . . . without a glance back at the girl. He had forgotten he was leaving her there." Calixta, left alone thus abruptly, lets Bobinôt walk her home and volunteers that if he still wants to marry her, "I don' care, me" (226), thus making the young Acadian man indescribably happy. And at about the same time Clarisse is telling Alcée that she loves him, thus making the young Creole gentleman equally ecstatic.

The reader knows that both men have been treated only coldly by their chosen brides. Why, then, do Bobinôt and Alcée feel such joy to be marrying Calixta and Clarisse? Both couples, again, have much in common in terms of social status and life-styles. But these men do not wish to marry other women who share these elements with them, so why Calixta and Clarisse, who clearly feel no passion for their prospective husbands? Surely at least part of the answer must lie in the feeling of each that he has won a prized possession, one that any man in similar circumstances would be proud to "own." Bobinôt and Alcée demonstrate, too, that such possessiveness may motivate the humble as well as the aristocratic man. In a later story, "Her Letters," a similar feeling, which Chopin then calls "the man-instinct of possession" (401), drives a widowed husband to distraction and finally to suicide by drowning.

"Désirée's Baby," Chopin's most famous story, also pivots around male possessiveness and related matters of identity. First, the foundling Désirée appears at the Valmondes' plantation with no identity at all; but the family accepts her affectionately, and she finds there a secure place and abundant love. When she grows up, however, and becomes the object of Armand Aubigny's love, her foster father reminds the young man that the girl is "nameless." But Armand declares himself indifferent to that fact: "What did it matter about a name when he could give her one of the oldest and proudest in Louisiana?" (241).

The question of identity arises again when Madame Valmondé looks at Désirée's month-old child and exclaims, "This is not the baby!" (241). The older woman then asks Désirée what Armand thinks of the child, and the happy young mother glowingly replies, "Oh, Armand is the proudest father in the parish, I believe, chiefly because it is a boy, to bear his name" (242).

The fact that the infant has Negro forebears gradually becomes apparent to everyone, last of course to Désirée. When she realizes the situation, Désirée demands of Armand, "look at our child. What does it mean? tell me." And he answers coldly, "It means . . . that the child is not white; it means that you are not white" (243). And, if she "is not white," of course, Armand Aubigny's pride in having Désirée and their son to bear his name has turned to bitter ashes.

Désirée writes to Madame Valmondé, begging her, "For God's sake tell them it is not true. You must know it is not true." If her racial identity is reestablished, Désirée believes that she will be able to resume her former place in her husband's affections. The older woman, however, replies briefly: "My own Désirée: Come home to Valmondé; back to your mother who loves you. Come with your child" (243). But when Armand tells her that he wants her to go, Désirée feels that the world really has no place for her and her baby. So she takes the infant and walks into the swamp, never to return.

Eventually Armand discovers that the black ancestry comes from himself and not from Désirée, thus concluding the story with an ironic reversal that demonstrates powerfully the irrationality of racism.

This reversal also points up an interesting fact about Chopin's view of the respective places of man and woman in the world. Désirée certainly understands that if she has an "untainted" bloodline, as she attempts to establish and as the physical evidence clearly suggests she does have, then Aubigny must necessarily have a "tainted" one. Yet, although functioning within the same bigoted tradition that causes Armand to send her coldly away to perish, Désirée wants only to regain her place as the beloved wife of this "tainted" man and the mother of his child of mixed blood.

Further, at no time does the truth occur to anyone except Désirée herself, again despite the clear physical evidence apparent to anyone who might really look at the two parents. Manifestly, in Chopin's view of life as revealed here Désirée, even leaving out of consideration her past status as a foundling, has far more to lose than Aubigny does, because her place and even her name depend upon a man's regarding her as a prized possession. Had the truth been known in time, Armand's pride would still have been wounded, but surely he would not have been destroyed, as Désirée and the baby are.

"Is Man [or Woman] No More Than This?"

Chopin, then, seems already in this first collection of short stories, sentimental and superficial as many of them are, to be moving toward the study of women in search of themselves. Even though Désirée and several others do find a sufficient sense of identity in viewing themselves as prized possessions of the men to whom they belong, in a few of the stories in Chopin's next volume the inevitable dissatisfaction with such a place in life will begin to emerge. And in the third collection, "A Vocation and a Voice," this dissatisfaction will become the dominant theme of the best stories.

But Chopin's interest, even in these earliest stories, extends well beyond the "woman-question" to encompass the entire, complex matter of human identity, memorably expressed by Shakespeare's Lear when he stands naked on the heath in the center of the tempest crying "Is man no more than this?"[8] Whether describing self-reliant young girls, analyzing the lingering dislocations of the Civil War, portraying emancipated black people who deny their freedom, examining the effects of love upon individual human personalities, or exploring the phenomenon of masculine possessiveness, Chopin creates in the stories of Bayou Folk characters struggling to fulfill the needs for self-knowledge, for love, and especially for a place in life where they can feel they belong.

Chapter Four
A Night in Acadie

In her second volume of stories, *A Night in Acadie,* Chopin shifts emphases and concentrates particularly on love—all kinds of love: filial, fraternal, paternal, maternal, marital, sexual—although she continues to examine the various other facets of human identity as well.

"Think of the Children, Edna"

Nine of the twenty-one stories center around children. Orrick Johns in a 1911 review of Chopin's *Bayou Folk* and *A Night in Acadie* says, "no such knowledge of children and no such love of them is to be found in other books."[1] This evidence that Chopin knew and loved children should be considered when analyzing Edna's ambivalent attitude toward her young sons in *The Awakening.* The children in the *Acadie* stories affect the lives of adults in varied ways. They heal, pacify, enlighten, comfort, and love. Even when they act mischievously, good often results.

In "After the Winter," for example, the interference of children brings M'sieur Michel, the protagonist, back into contact with humanity after twenty-five years of alienation. "Ripe Figs" reveals beautifully the differing perspectives on time of the child and the adult, expressing in one short page virtually the essence of the generation gap. And "A Matter of Prejudice" tells of a proud Creole woman who for ten years had refused to visit her son Henri because he is married to an "American" woman. Finally, a child's love heals this breach between the generations.

"Mamouche" carries the name of one of its central characters, a mischievous waif who turns up one rainy night at Doctor John-Luis's door and eventually brings to that bachelor physician the fulfillment he had not even known he lacked. Mamouche also figures in bringing fulfillment to two adults in "The Lilies" when he lets down the fences that separate the Widow Angèle's calf from Mr. Billy's crops. The crops suffer, but the story ends with a hint that marriage between the impoverished Widow and the wealthy but lonely Mr. Billy may follow.

"Odalie Misses Mass" tells of a little girl who stops by to "show herself" dressed up for mass on Assumption day to Aunt Pinky, her "old friend and protegée" (406). Finding that the ill, old black woman has been left alone while everyone else has gone to church, Odalie stays with her. After mass Odalie's mother finds both the child and the old woman asleep; but Aunt Pinky never awakens. Odalie's childish conceit, her obvious delight in displaying her new outfit, and the love that makes her miss the big occasion after all rather than leave Aunt Pinky alone—these qualities illustrate what Johns means in saying that Chopin knew and loved children.

Two stories develop the idea that a woman needs to feel maternal love, even if she has never borne a child. In "Polydore" Mamzelle Adelaide—a kind, naive, middle-aged spinster—tries faithfully to fulfill her promise made years before to Polydore's dying mother to look after the boy. Now a stupid, lazy lad of fourteen, Polydore pretends one day to be ill, thus causing Mamzelle to go out into the heat and consequently to develop a severe fever. Polydore feels dreadfully guilty. At last he confesses to Mamzelle "in a way that bared his heart to her for the first time. . . . she felt as if a kind of miracle had happened. . . . She knew that a bond of love had been forged. . . . she drew him close to her and kissed him as mothers kiss" (417). Thus through maternal love Mamzelle's good but heretofore emotionally impoverished life gains warmth and beauty.

"Regret" develops more fully this theme that to experience life richly a woman needs a child or children to love and care for. Although in the beginning Mamzelle Aurélie, the protagonist, feels perfectly satisfied, circumstances force her to recognize that her life lacks something.

Mamzelle, one of Chopin's most memorable women, "possessed a good strong figure, ruddy cheeks, . . . and a determined eye. She wore a man's hat . . . and an old blue army overcoat . . . and sometimes topboots." Far from regretting her spinster status, "Mamzelle Aurélie had never thought of marrying. . . . and at the age of fifty she had not yet lived to regret it." Neither does she think of herself as lonely, although "she was quite alone in the world, except for her dog Ponto, and the negroes . . . and the fowls, a few cows, a couple of mules, her gun . . . and her religion" (375). But when her neighbor Odile must go away on an emergency, Mamzelle offers to care for Odile's children.

Mamzelle soon discovers that "children are not little pigs; they require . . . attentions which were wholly unexpected by Mamzelle Aurélie, and which she was ill prepared to give." In time she learns that "Marcélette always wept when spoken to in a loud and commanding tone" (376), that Ti Nomme picks all the choicest flowers in the garden and cannot sleep without being told at least one story, that Elodie must be rocked and sung to sleep—in short that each child is an individual and that each must have all the privileges and attention that individuality involves. In fact, Mamzelle confides to her cook: "I tell you . . . I'd rather manage a dozen plantation' than fo' chil'ren. It's terrassent! Bonté! Don't talk to me about chil'ren" (377).

The spinster quickly adjusts, however. She learns to accept Ti Nomme's "moist kisses—the expressions of an affectionate and exuberant nature." In a few days she becomes accustomed "to the laughing, the crying, the chattering." And by the end of two weeks, "she could sleep comfortably with little Elodie's hot plump body pressed close against her" (377).

But then Odile reclaims her brood. Mamzelle watches them leave: "The excitement was all over. . . . How still it was when they were gone!" She goes back into the house, now empty as never before: "The evening shadows were creeping and deepening around her solitary figure. She let her head fall down upon her bended arm, and began to cry. . . . She cried like a man, with sobs that seemed to tear her very soul" (378). Mamzelle again lacks that important part of a woman's life, the maternal relationship; but worse, perhaps, she can never again perceive herself as the strong, self-sufficient, satisfied planter.

Self-Sacrificing Love

Five of the stories in A Night in Acadie feature unselfish characters who sacrifice themselves for someone they love. In "A Dresden Lady in Dixie," a little Acadian girl named Agapie hides a beautiful Dresden figurine from the big plantation house in her soapbox full of treasures. After it is found there everyone is heartbroken, especially Agapie and her family. But then Pa-Jeff, an old black man to whom Agapie has been kind, learns of the crisis. Sympathizing with her and her family in their shame and feeling secure in his own reputation for utter honesty, Pa-Jeff makes up a story about himself as the center of a controversy between "De Sperrit" and "Satan." "Satan," he says, made him take the figurine and hide it in the child's box; but "De Sperrit" moves him to confess his "guilt" and clear the child's name. Consequently, "Agapie grew up to deserve the confidence and favors of the family. She redoubled her acts of kindness toward Pa-Jeff; but somehow she could not look into his face again" (351). Although sentimentality mars this story, Agapie's suffering could have been portrayed so vividly only by a writer who understood and loved children.

The protagonist in "Tante Cat'rinette" acts from a love as unselfish as Pa-Jeff's. While still a slave Cat'rinette had saved the life of her master's daughter, and the father in gratitude had named the daughter "Cat'rine

. . . Das Miss Kitty" (337), freed Cat'rinette, and given her a house. But now, thirty-five years later, things have changed. Miss Kitty lives in poverty, and the town has condemned Tante Cat'rinette's house, wanting to pay her $1,000 and then demolish it. The old woman, however, refuses to sell and fears that mysterious powers will destroy her house if she leaves it even for a moment. But one day she learns that Miss Kitty is seriously ill and too poor to hire a physician.

That night very late, Cat'rinette dares to leave her house to visit the woman she deeply loves. Miss Kitty, drowsing restlessly, reacts "instinctively" to Cat'rinette's touch: "'It's Tante Cat'rinette!' she exclaimed. . . . 'They all said you wouldn' come'" (342). The old woman stays all night, caring for Miss Kitty and the baby and thus enabling both Miss Kitty and her husband, Mr. Raymond, to get a few hours of rest. Just before daybreak she leaves, to return home before those fearful forces can seize her house. But she promises to return each night.

On her way home Tante Cat'rinette has a vision in which "Vieumaite," an image of her old master, tells her to take the city's offer, lend the money to Mr. Raymond, move into Miss Kitty's home where she can care for the younger woman properly, live there until she dies, and then by her will leave whatever remains of the $1,000 to Miss Kitty. Thus Cat'rinette's love for Miss Kitty leads her to solve everyone's problems. The little house she had received as a mark of honor long ago now has become a symbol of her importance to the family she loves and with whom she feels she belongs.

"Nég Creole" is another story about a self-sacrificing former slave who finds life meaningful only through his relationship with the last survivor of the family that once owned him. Mamzelle Aglaé, that survivor, lives in abject poverty, complains constantly, and appreciates not at all what Chicot, the ex-slave, does for her. Chicot sympathizes with Mamzelle and scrounges food for her, but feels deep shame for her fallen state. In both of these miserable creatures, caste pride remains undiminished despite decades of deprivation and humiliation. Both depend upon each other for their sense of who they are, because in a sense they had ceased to "be" when their old place in life vanished.

In "Ozème's Holiday" Chopin illustrates unselfish love while also revealing the importance of image to Ozème, an Acadian plantation hand. Although a hard worker, he values his reputation as a happy-go-lucky fellow. One October day, when the cotton is bursting in the fields, he sets out for a week's vacation on Cane River. Along the way, however, he discovers an old black woman and her son who are both ill; so he spends his week picking their cotton for them. Yet when he gets home, he makes up a story about the "sporting time" he has had. Ozème's compassion for down-and-out strangers causes him to sacrifice his own interests. Yet he acts irresponsibly in timing his vacation and he lies in telling about his week's "sporting" activities in order to maintain his image as a devil-may-care fellow.

Gilma, the nineteen-year-old orphan in "Dead Men's Shoes," shares with Ozème unselfishness and the need for a stable concept of himself. Gilma has lived for ten years with Gamiche, helping the lonely old planter and developing a deep filial love for him, even though no blood relationship exists. Gamiche has just died, leaving a nephew, Septime; a widowed niece, Ma'me Brozé; and Ma'me Brozé's two little girls. Although the relatives do not even attend Gamiche's funeral, they immediately take possession of his farm and move Gilma's personal possessions out of the house. Grief stricken, homeless, enraged, Gilma saddles his horse to leave, only to be stopped by Septime, who claims that even the horse belongs to Gamiche's heirs.

Determined to prove his ownership of the horse, Gilma goes to Gamiche's lawyer for help and there learns that Gamiche had willed everything to him, his son in love though not in flesh. Gilma, of course, feels "stunned, drunk, with the sudden joy of possession. . . . He felt like another being who would have to readjust himself to the new conditions" (422–23). But learning to feel that he is that other being, not merely that he is "like another being," proves difficult. "A subtle uneasiness, a self-dissatisfaction had mingled with his elation" (424). Finally he decides to return to his earlier status, that of homeless boy, and leave the farm with "Mr. Gamiche's own flesh an' blood" (425). Although Chopin has Gilma act in response to his own need for continuity instead of self-sacrificing love like that evidenced by Ozème and several other characters, the ending nevertheless seems unlikely and even rather maudlin.

"Cavanelle," an interesting study of fraternal love, tells how one man brings meaning and purpose to his own existence by giving himself to another. The protagonist, Cavanelle, loving as selflessly as Pa-Jeff, Tante Cat'rinette, Chicot, and Ozème, dedicates himself to his ill sister, Mathilde, whom he believes to be a great singer. The narrator, shocked at Mathilde's pathetic musical performance and Cavanelle's seeming deafness, wonders, "is Cavanelle a fool? is he a lunatic?" But then she answers her own questions: "I realized that Cavanelle loved Mathilde intensely, and we all know that love is blind, but a god just the same" (372). Cavanelle, like Chopin's other self-sacrificing characters, acts from a deep, fulfilling, humane kind of love.

32 KATE CHOPIN

Some Strange Romances

The seven remaining stories in *A Night in Acadie* focus primarily on romantic love, and some of them feature strange relationships indeed. A few are little more than sketches. For example, "Caline" simply paints a portrait of a young country girl whose perception of life is changed forever by a passing train. When it develops mechanical problems near where she lies asleep, a young man gets off, paints her portrait, and then resumes his journey. Soon she goes to the city and begins to look into the face of every passerby, seeking the face that "awakened" her that day.

The title story of the volume, "A Night in Acadie," portrays a girl named Zaïda, who in her headstrong determination to live her own life foreshadows Edna Pontellier. The protagonist, a young bachelor named Telèsphore, meets Zaïda on a train and decides to go with her to Foché's ball. The way the girl moves and acts captures Telèsphore's interest: "She carried herself boldly" with "an absence of reserve . . . yet . . . no lack of womanliness" (487). Yet later when he "tried to think of her he could not think at all. . . . his brain was not so occupied with her as his senses were" (489). Zaïda in her bold, sensuous ways and in her effect on Telèsphore reminds the reader a bit of Calixta as Chopin portrayed her in 1892 in "At the 'Cadian Ball,'" but she suggests more forcefully the 1898 Calixta in "The Storm."[2]

As events develop, Telèsphore learns that Zaïda plans to run away and marry a rascal named André Pascal. Unable to stop her, Telèsphore goes along to prevent her riding alone at midnight to "Wat Gibson's—a kine of justice of the peace or something" (494), where Zaïda says the wedding is scheduled for 1:00 A.M. Arriving at the trysting place, they learn that André has been drinking and "sho' raisin' de ole Nick" all day "down to de P'int" (496).

Eventually, drunk and belligerent, André arrives. Zaïda declares, "You might stan' yere till the day o' judgement on yo' knees befo' me; I ain't neva goin' to marry you." And he retorts insultingly, "The hell you ain't!" (497). Immediately, Telèsphore knocks Pascal down, whereupon Pascal tries to draw his gun but drops it. Zaïda picks it up and lays it on the table. "She was going to see fair play," the narrator declares. The two men fight fiercely: "The brute instinct that drives men at each other's throat was awake and stirring in these two. . . . [Zaïda] did not raise her voice or lift her finger to stay the combat. . . . only her eyes seemed to be alive and burning and blazing" (497).

Thus she watches the combat in the highest excitement, doing nothing to prevent the maiming or even death of either combatant, determined "to see fair play" between the man she had only that day met and the insulting drunk she had meant to marry despite the objections of family and friends. Zaïda's attitude toward the fight has some of the intense detachment that forms a strange part of Edna Pontellier's attitude toward life.

In an anticlimactic denouement, Telèsphore, after winning the fight, asserts his masculine authority and drives Zaïda home. Zaïda "was like a little child and followed whither he led" (499). Chopin apparently modified this story in an attempt to please R. W. Gilder, influential editor of the *Century*. She wrote to him: "I have made certain alterations which you thought the story required to give it artistic or ethical value. . . . The marriage is omitted, and the girl's character softened and tempered by her rude experience."[3] The original ending having been lost, one can only speculate on its content; but it seems to have been less edifying and more consistent with Zaïda's character. At any rate, this bold, sensuous, self-assertive girl exhibits until the end of the fight qualities suggestive of both the voluptuous Calixta and the headstrong Edna Pontellier.

Another strange romance is that of Mamzelle Fleurette, the heroine in "A Sentimental Soul." Robert Arner calls Mamzelle "As unlikely a rebel as anyone may wish to meet."[4] A devoutly religious spinster, Mamzelle falls secretly in love with a married man, Lacodie, who loudly voices his radical political opinions and intentions to overcharge the prosperous. "Much older than he, much taller," Mamzelle "held no opinions" (388). She does believe such extra charges to the wealthy to be "far from right. . . . But she held a vague understanding that . . . ungodliness was constitutional with [men], like their sex" (389).

Mamzelle's appearance reflects her pinched, repressed existence: "the black alpaca skirt . . . hung in long nun-like folds around her spare figure. . . . Her sleek hair was painfully and suspiciously black. . . . There was little . . . in her withered face, except a pathetic . . . appeal to be permitted to exist." But her behavior as she walks toward the cathedral one day hints at turmoil inside: "When she passed the locksmith's shop over the way and heard his voice within, she grew tremulously self-conscious, fingering her veil, swishing the black alpaca" (389).

Mamzelle seems as unlikely to be a lover as a rebel, but through her Chopin creates her most beautiful description of falling in love: "Mamzelle Fleurette was in . . . trouble . . . so bitter, so sweet, so bewildering, so terrifying! . . . She thought the world was growing brighter and more beautiful; she thought the flowers had redoubled their sweetness and the birds their song, and that the voices of her fellow-creatures had grown kinder and their faces truer" (389).

Recognizing her problem at last, Mamzelle hurries to confession, where she shocks the priest: "A slap in the face would not have startled Father Fochelle more forcibly." Determining that Lacodie is unaware of Mamzelle's love for him, the priest scolds her and tells her to "keep Satan at bay" (391).

Soon Lacodie develops a fever and dies. Father Fochelle forbids that Mamzelle even go to the funeral, "and she did not question his authority, or his ability to master the subtleties of a situation utterly beyond reach of her own powers" (394). She keeps Lacodie's picture, which she had clipped from a newspaper, hidden from herself in a big dictionary. But love overpowers Mamzelle. She confesses: "I try, but I cannot help it. To love him is like breathing. . . . I pray, and pray, and it does no good, for half of my prayers are for the repose of his soul. It surely cannot be a sin, to pray for the repose of his soul?" (394). The priest, however, disagrees.

In the meantime Lacodie's young, pretty widow has begun taking in washing to support herself and her child. Spring comes. She grows flowers and buys a bird. Then she begins to sing with the bird. Soon she marries again.

The widow's remarriage shakes Mamzelle's very soul: "A terrible upheaval [was] taking place in [her] soul. She was preparing for the first time in her life to take her conscience into her own keeping." And so, Mamzelle Fleurette becomes a rebel as well as a lover. She goes to a church across town from her own neighborhood and confesses to a priest she does not know. She tells him "all her little venial sins, which she had much difficulty in bringing to a number of any dignity," but she does not mention "her love for Lacodie, the dead husband of another woman." After confession, "Mamzelle Fleurette did not ride back to her home; she walked. The sensation of walking on air was altogether delicious; she had never experienced it before" (396). That feeling of "walking on air" does not come to Mamzelle when she first feels love for a man, delightful as she finds that experience; only when she takes "her conscience into her own keeping" does she experience it. Thus Mamzelle's need for autonomy in making her own decisions and choices becomes a minor theme in "A Sentimental Soul."

In "At Chênière Caminada," another story of thwarted love, a shy young fisherman named Tonie falls in love with Claire Duvigné—a beautiful, popular girl who, like Lacodie, dies. Far from grieving for her as Mamzelle does for Lacodie, however, Tonie rejoices because now Claire will not marry anyone else. An instinctive coquette, Claire had sensed Tonie's unspoken passion one day when she hired a ride in his boat. But "She did not dream that under the rude, calm exterior . . . his reason [was] yielding to the savage instinct of his blood" (314). As a matter of fact, Tonie had come very close to killing both Claire and himself while they were alone on the lake that day. Apparently Chopin was already associating death in the ocean with human passion in 1893, five years before Edna Pontellier would yield her body to the erotic embrace of the sea in *The Awakening*.

The development of a strange and consuming passion also provides the central interest of "Azélie," another 1893 story. 'Polyte falls in love with Azélie, a poor Acadian girl who presents quite a contrast to Claire Duvigné: "The face was colorless but for the red, curved line of the lips. . . . her black hair was plastered smooth back. . . . There was no trace of . . . coquetry in her manner. He resented this as a token of indifference toward his sex" (291). 'Polyte at first dislikes Azélie; then he wishes she would go away; then he asks her to marry him; and finally he quits a good job to follow her and her family when they move away. What 'Polyte feels for Azélie, like Tonie's passion for Claire, might more properly be called lust than love, but Chopin in this volume seems to be studying all shades of "love," including unrequited physical attraction.

Finally, two stories feature wives who experience difficulty in abiding by their marriage vows. In "A Respectable Woman" Mrs. Baroda is a happily married woman who feels "a little provoked" about her husband's friend Gouvernail visiting their plantation at a time when "She was looking forward to a period of . . . undisturbed tête-à-tête with her husband" (333). But she finds Gouvernail disturbingly attractive, despite her strong love for her husband. In fact, her passion for the guest almost overwhelms her one evening when she encounters him in the garden: "Her physical being was for the moment predominant. . . . She wanted to reach out . . . and touch him with the sensitive tips of her fingers. . . . She wanted to draw close to him and whisper against his cheek . . . as she might have done if she had not been a respectable woman" (335). Recognizing what is happening, she escapes to the city and remains there until he leaves the plantation. The narrator says: "Mrs. Baroda was greatly tempted . . . to tell her husband—who was also her friend—of this folly. . . . But she did not. . . . she knew there are some battles in life which a human being must fight alone" (335–36). In this story, written in January 1894, Mrs. Baroda evidences no romantic naïveté and no lack of sexual satisfaction within her marriage, two commonly suggested motives for the infidelity of Edna in *The Awakening*.[5] She simply feels strong sexual attraction toward another man besides her husband. She has no motivation for being unfaithful except a physically healthy body. On the contrary, she has every reason for being faithful to her beloved husband.

And of course she does flee the scene to make sure that she remains faithful. But before the year's end, she suggests that Gouvernail be invited for another visit. Her husband declares his delight that she has "overcome" her "dislike" for his friend. She laughingly tells him, "after pressing a long, tender kiss upon his lips, 'I have overcome everything! . . . This time I shall be very nice to him'" (336). And the reader understands that she is going to risk losing everything—her husband, her marriage, her very happiness—simply because passion aroused demands its fulfillment.

"Athénaïse" is another story about marriage from a woman's perspective. The protagonist, Athénaïse, has recently married Cazeau, a soft-spoken but severe-looking widower. When his bride does not return one evening after visiting her parents, "He did not worry much about Athénaïse . . . ; his chief solicitude was manifestly for the pony she had ridden" (426). Cazeau, being very busy, has little time to concern himself about Athénaïse's absence, but on the third afternoon after her departure "the task of bringing his wife back to a sense of her duty" (428) becomes even more important than his other work. Cazeau realizes that "The marriage had been a blunder; he had only to look into her eyes to feel that, to discover her growing aversion" (427). But he expects to make the best of the situation and to see to it that Athénaïse does the same.

Meanwhile, Athénaïse, younger than Cazeau, less experienced, and miserable in the married state, has returned to her parents' home and announced that she will never return to her husband's: "The announcement had scattered consternation, as she knew it would. She had been implored, scolded, entreated, stormed at. . . . Why in the name of God had she married Cazeau? Her father had lashed her with the question a dozen times." Of course, her father's question only matches her own: "Why indeed? It was difficult now for her to understand why, unless because she supposed it was customary for girls to marry when the right opportunity came. Cazeau, she knew, would make life more comfortable for her; and again, she had liked him, and had even been rather flustered when he pressed her hands and kissed them" (430). Thus the reasons that led Athénaïse into marriage sound similar to those that almost led Euphrasie to marry Placide in "A No-Account Creole" and that will later lead Edna into her tragic marriage in *The Awakening*.

Athénaïse explains to her uncomprehending family that she does not dislike her husband but simply the condition of being married: "It's jus' being married that I detes' an' despise. I hate being Mrs. Cazeau, an' would want to be Athénaïse Miché again" (431). She still sees herself as Athénaïse Miché, the young girl she had been until two months before; and she finds it impossible to perceive herself as Mrs. Cazeau, a married woman with a completely new role to play in life and even a new name to which she must learn to answer.

When confronted by her husband on the third day of her truancy, Athénaïse "appeared neither angry nor frightened, but thoroughly unhappy, with an appeal in her soft dark eyes . . . that wounded and maddened him at once. But whatever he might feel, Cazeau knew only one way to act toward a woman" (431). He simply tells her what to do. And confronted thus, Athénaïse yields helplessly: "Her husband's . . . mere presence, brought to her a sudden sense of hopelessness, . . . of the futility of rebellion against a social and sacred institution" (432). Cazeau, in knowing "only one way to act"—to tell Athénaïse what to do—foreshadows Léonce's first response to Edna's rebellion in *The Awakening.* Cazeau's basic kindliness and decency also resemble those of Léonce. And further, the young wife's hopelessness also predicts a scene in the later story when Edna throws her wedding ring onto the floor and stomps it with her foot.

Some sense of how Athénaïse feels comes to Cazeau, however, as they ride home: "The sight of a great solitary oak-tree . . . brought vividly back to Cazeau . . . a scene of many years ago," when he had been a small boy. He and his father were on horseback, returning a runaway slave to their plantation: "Black Gabe was moving on before them at a little dog-trot. . . . They had halted beneath this big oak to enable the negro to take breath; for Cazeau's father was a kind . . . master, and every one had agreed . . . that Black Gabe was a fool . . . for wanting to run away from him" (432–33). The memory makes Cazeau distinctly uncomfortable, and he resolves that never again will he force Athénaïse to return to him: "For the companionship of no woman on earth would he again undergo the humiliating sensation of baseness that had overtaken him in passing the old oak-tree" (438). Thus Chopin specifically links the institution of marriage as practiced in 1895 with the institution of slavery.

The girl does flee again; but this time she goes to New Orleans rather than to her father's home. Cazeau "knew that he could again compel her return . . . but the loss of self-respect seemed to him too dear a price to pay for a wife" (438). So he does not attempt to contact her.

Athénaïse spends a rather lonely month in New Orleans, but the "com-

forting, comfortable sense of not being married" (444) makes up for the
loneliness. Her neighbor in the boarding house happens to be Gouvernail,
the same bachelor who attracts Mrs. Baroda in "A Respectable Woman."
He helps Athénaïse to pass the time, and she drifts toward a probable love
affair with him: "He was patient; . . . That she was married made no . . .
difference to Gouvernail. . . . When the time came that she wanted
him, . . . he felt he would have a right to her. So long as she did not want
him, he had no right to her,—no more than her husband had" (450). Perhaps some of Gouvernail's attractiveness to women results from his feeling,
unusual in Chopin's male characters, that women have the right to want a
man or not.

At any rate, the discovery that she is pregnant saves Athénaïse from
being awakened sexually by Gouvernail. The news transforms her completely: "Her whole being was steeped in a wave of ecstasy. When she . . .
looked at herself in the mirror, a face met hers which she seemed to see for
the first time, so transfigured was it with wonder." Learning to view herself as mother seems much easier for Athénaïse than learning to view herself as wife. She thinks: "Cazeau must know. As she thought of him, the
first purely sensuous tremor of her life swept over her. . . . She was impa-
tient to be with him. Her whole passionate nature was aroused as if by a
miracle" (451). She takes the earliest train home to Cazeau, and on the
long trip she "could think of nothing but him." When she arrives, "he felt
the yielding of her whole body against him. He felt her lips for the first
time respond to the passion of his own" (454). Thus Athénaïse finds that
prospective motherhood not only offers a role in which she feels comfortable but also releases her pent-up love for Cazeau.

Yet she has paid a price for fulfilling these two emotional needs. She has
sacrificed her name and more; she has sacrificed also her autonomy, her
right to live as a discrete individual. Athénaïse Miché exists no longer.

Chapter Five
"A Vocation and a Voice"

In Chopin's third collection of stories, the proposed but unpublished "A Vocation and a Voice,"[1] the characterizations become firm, and the drive toward autonomy becomes insistent in many characters. As Robert Arner points out, had this collection been published Chopin's works probably would not have been neglected as they have been, for these stories exhibit "a strength and a maturity, a firmness of line and a level of artistic achievement"[2] that critics would have found difficult to ignore. Most of these stories turn inward, studying human emotions and values more deeply than do the stories in *Bayou Folk* and *A Night in Acadie*. They treat a number of topics—religion, suicide, illusions, the fickleness of people and of fate, the power of sex, and the impulse toward self-assertion. And most look deeply into some character or human experience, trying to fathom exactly what comprises the fulfilled person or the adequate life.

Religion

Five of the stories indicate that Chopin was thinking about religion—its significance, scope, and meaning to the human psyche.[3] Two of these, "An Idle Fellow" and "A Scrap and a Sketch," espouse a sort of Emersonian nature religion; the other three insist that the fully realized person needs to experience harmony among his or her sensual, sensuous, and spiritual parts.

The narrator in "An Idle Fellow," a "bookworm," describes the wisdom of Paul, who sits drinking "the scent of the clover" and reading in the eyes of passersby "the story of their souls" (280). Paul personifies Emerson's concepts of the relative value of books and nature as teachers of the self[4] and interprets a bird's song much like the one Whitman "translates" in "Out of the Cradle Endlessly Rocking."[5]

"The Night Came Slowly" shares with "An Idle Fellow" this theme of the powers of nature. The narrator, wanting "neither books nor men," asks: "Can one of them talk to me like . . . the Summer night? . . . My whole being was abandoned to the soothing and penetrating charm of the night" (366). But a man and his "Bible Class" come into the woods and break the spell. The narrator sneers: "What does he know of Christ? . . . I would rather ask the stars: they have seen him" (366). So only nature can teach with authority.

Chopin joins "The Night Came Slowly" with "Juanita" by publishing them under one title, "A Scrap and a Sketch," and by proposing to present them together again in this third collection under the title "Sketches," thus suggesting that the reader should look for a thematic link between the two. That the stories are related is further suggested by the fact that both appear as diary entries within a two-day period in July 1894.[6]

Juanita, a two-hundred-pound girl dressed in a dirty "Mother Hubbard," mysteriously attracts men from far and near—among others a city gentleman, a wealthy Missouri farmer, a Texas millionaire. But one day a poor, shabby, one-legged beggar appears. Juanita bears his child out of wedlock and "lavishes . . . her undivided affections" (368) upon him. Love thus proves again to be a strange force, indeed, and a woman's soul as unfathomable as the universe. That Chopin links "Juanita" with "The Night Came Slowly" emphasizes the naturalness of sex and the fact that it, like other aspects of nature, exerts a force so vast, complex, and mysterious as to defy comprehension, much less control, by human creatures.

"An Idle Fellow" and "A Scrap and a Sketch" suggest that, to hear the "language of God," one must listen to nature. But Archibald, the protagonist in "A Morning Walk," receives in the church important truths about himself. As a scientist he lives close to nature, but it has never spoken to him the "language of God" until one spring morning when he follows a lovely young girl named Lucy to church and hears the minister preach on the words of Jesus, "I am the Resurrection and the Life." Archibald can understand when the preacher speaks "the language of God," not only because he has long been intimate with nature but also because Lucy has stirred his sensuous and sensual feelings on this lovely spring morning. With the preacher's text comes a "vision of life . . . the poet's vision, of the life that is within and the life that is without, pulsing in unison, breathing the harmony of an undivided existence" (569). How different from the way Edna would feel in *The Awakening:* "She had all her life long been accustomed to harbor thoughts and emotions which never voiced themselves. . . . They belonged to her and were her own. They . . . concerned no one but herself" (929). And only in death will she find a way to bring "the life that is within" into harmonious unison with "the life that is without." But for Archibald, the sensuous, the sensual, and the spiritual come together in harmony, making it possible for him to embrace all of experience.

The other two stories that treat religion, "Two Portraits" and "Lilacs," portray women who, unlike Archibald, find it impossible to breathe "the harmony of an undivided existence." Chopin had earlier given other titles to "Two Portraits," at one time calling it "The Nun and the Wanton" and at another "The Nun, the Wife and the Wanton" (1026). All three titles, of course, suggest that the protagonist, Alberta, exists in a divided state. This story emphasizes the maternal influence in determining the sort of person a child becomes.

Chopin first sketches the character of Alberta the Wanton, a young woman whose substitute mother, a prostitute, alternates between beating Alberta and indulging the child's every whim. Alberta also becomes a prostitute at an early age, and she takes good care of her body "for she knows it brings her love to squander and gold to squander" (463). Someone tells Alberta to save her gold, warning her that she will not always remain young and beautiful. But Alberta, like a good many Chopin characters, knows a way to escape that which she cannot face: "with death and oblivion always within her reach" she need never fear the "degradation" of age and "ugliness" (463). Alberta the Wanton, possessing no spiritual dimension, can end her existence whenever the "ugliness" of age threatens "degradation."

After completing her portrait of Alberta the Wanton, Chopin puts the same raw materials into a different environment and creates by contrast Alberta the Nun, who needs a physical dimension as badly as her twin needs a spiritual one. Whenever the child tries to experience God with her senses, the mother figure tells her that one reaches God with the soul, not the body. This "holy woman" teaches Alberta "that the soul must be made perfect and the flesh subdued" (464). Consequently, when this Alberta matures, she feels an overpowering impulse toward the spiritual; and so she enters the convent, where she sees "visions" that seem to be at least as sensual as they are spiritual. Their effects are described through such terms as "ecstacy," "roused," "awakened," "pressed her lips," "quivering contemplation," "abandon herself," and "swooned in rapture" (465–66). Thus Alberta the Nun, with her attention riveted upon heaven, remains as pathetically unfulfilled as Alberta the Wanton, whose total existence centers upon the flesh. Both lack a necessary dimension.

"Lilacs" develops a theme much like that of "Two Portraits'" but in it different individuals embody the Wanton and the Nun and each comes to realize what her life lacks. The protagonist, Mme. Adrienne Farival, parallels the Wanton, although Chopin develops Adrienne's character more fully than Alberta's. Adrienne—an actress, singer, object of devotion to a series of men—lives an exciting, glamorous life. But every spring when the lilacs first bloom, she goes to visit the convent where she once attended school. She arrives with an armload of lilacs and an expensive gift for the convent; and she remains for two weeks, her pleasure in the quiet peacefulness revealing that her worldly life lacks something important. Sister Agathe, approximating Alberta the Nun, looks forward to Adrienne's visits from one lilac-time to the next, declaring that "If you should once fail to come, it would be like spring coming without the sunshine or the song of birds" (358). Her joy at the light and life associated with Adrienne reveals the incompleteness of convent life.

But one spring the Mother Superior, apparently having heard about Adrienne's worldly life, writes a cold message forbidding Adrienne to enter again the convent's premises. When Adrienne arrives with her lilacs, a messenger silently hands her the letter and then closes the doors in her face. Consequently, Adrienne and Sister Agathe both suffer greatly. Each needs that brief but nourishing contact with the other's world to fill a bit of the void that exists inside herself.

Fascination with Suicide

Perhaps Chopin felt that a person can fully control his or her own life only through the decisive act of ending it. At any rate, she created a number of suicidal characters, several of them in this group of stories. Alberta the Wanton, for example, knows that for the totally physical person escape through suicide always remains possible. When Chopin's characters do reach out to embrace "death and oblivion" (463), they usually choose to drown. In "Suzette," discussed more fully in the next chapter, the narrator hints that Michel has drowned himself. And in "An Egyptian Cigarette," the first-person narrator, after smoking a hallucinatory cigarette, describes an ambivalent, erotic hallucination of drowning:

I laughed at the oracles and scoffed at the stars when they told that after the rapture of life I would open my arms inviting death, and the waters would envelop me. . . .

The water! the water! In my eyes, my ears, my throat! It strangles me! Help! will the gods not help me?

Oh! the sweet rapture of rest! There is music in the Temple. And here is fruit to taste. (571–72)

Later a similarly ambivalent view of the engulfing waters, here attributed to a hallucination, will lose its dreamlike quality and become a central symbol in *The Awakening*.

Further, in "Her Letters," one of Chopin's most important stories, the protagonist does drown himself. "Her Letters" tells the story of a marriage, largely through a man's behavior and thoughts during a few years following his wife's death. The wife has lived a double life. To her husband, "She had never seemed . . . to have had a secret. . . . He knew her to have been cold and passionless, but true, and watchful of his . . . happiness" (401).

But in the first scene of the story, she fondles a bundle of letters. One she kisses "again and again. With her sharp white teeth she tore the far corner . . . where the name was written; she bit the torn scrap and tasted it." Only the letters remain of her affair with a man who "had changed the water in her veins to wine, whose taste had brought delirium" (399). For four years she has "been feeding upon [the letters] . . . they had sustained her . . . and kept her spirit from perishing" (398).

Yet she loves her husband, too. Knowing that she will soon die, "She shrank from inflicting the pain . . . which . . . those letters would bring . . . to one . . . whose tenderness and years of devotion had made him . . . dear." Finding herself unable to part with her treasured letters— "How desolate and empty would have been her remaining days without them" (399)—she arrives at a daring plan that reveals much about both her husband and herself. She wraps the bundle and on it writes: "I leave this package to the care of my husband. With perfect faith in his loyalty and his love, I ask him to destroy it unopened" (400).

His reaction when he finds the letters sheds light on the nature of both the man and the marriage: "If he had come upon that bundle of letters in the first flush of his poignant sorrow there would not have been an instant's hesitancy. To destroy it promptly and without question would have seemed a welcome expression of devotion—a way . . . of crying out his love." But she has been dead for a year before he finds the bundle, and so he at first feels mystified: "his face . . . spoke loyalty and honesty, and his eyes were as faithful as a dog's and as loving. . . . But he was slow. 'Destroy it unopened,' he re-read, half-aloud, 'but why unopened?'" Gradually, of course, the ensuing question comes to him: "What secret save one could a woman choose to have die with her?" And he now reacts rapidly: "As quickly as the suggestion came to his mind, so swiftly did the man-instinct of possession stir in his blood" (400–401).

Thus Chopin reveals with great subtlety that masculine possessiveness constitutes the pivotal problem with husband, wife, and marriage. In fact, Chopin treats such possessiveness in most of her best works about man-woman relationships, including "At the 'Cadian Ball," "In Sabine," "Désirée's Baby," "At Chênière Caminada," "Athénaïse," "The Story of an Hour," "Wiser Than a God," "The Gentleman from New Orleans," and of course *The Awakening*—in which the action is motivated by Edna's reaction to the possessiveness of Lèonce, Alcée, and finally Robert.

The husband in "Her Letters," nevertheless, does behave as his wife knew he would; that is, he destroys the letters, not by burning for fear that he might accidentally read a word or phrase as they burn, but by casting them into the river. He thereupon becomes a driven man, however, seeking the answer to his mystery in every conversation and contact. Finally, after years of such torture, "He no longer sought to know from men and women what they . . . could not tell him. Only the river knew. He went and stood again upon the bridge where . . . the darkness . . . had . . . engulfed his manhood" (405). And so, feeling that his "manhood" has been forever "engulfed" with the letters, he throws himself also into the water.

The river affects the widower in much the same hypnotic, erotic way that it affects the narrator in "An Egyptian Cigarette" and that the sea affects Edna in *The Awakening*. In "Her Letters,"

Only the river knew. . . . He could hear it promising him with caressing voice, peace and sweet repose. He could hear . . . the song of the water inviting him.

A moment more and he had gone to seek her, and to join her . . . in the immeasurable rest. (405)

In all three accounts, the sirens of the water seem to promise caresses, rapture, and peaceful repose to those who accept the invitation to shed their individuality (or, in Edna's case, the struggle to establish it) and become one with the elements.

Illusions

Three of the stories projected for "A Vocation and a Voice" focus on people's illusions—both the futility of illusions, on the one hand, and their power in an individual's life, on the other.

In "The White Eagle" the protagonist gropes her way through the misfortunes of a lonely life, always carrying with her an old cast-iron eagle that had "sheltered her unconscious dreams" (671) in childhood. Eventually she dies and someone places the eagle at the head of her grave, where he perches with a seemingly wise but actually vacuous look. The bird seems to symbolize the dreams, hopes, and illusions of the character. Although her dreams remain unfulfilled and in a sense as meaningless as the bird's expression, without them this woman would have been utterly alone and defenseless against life's misfortunes.

"Two Summers and Two Souls" links an ephemeral infatuation with a man's illusion that no commitment should ever be broken. The result is predictably tragic. A summer romance leads a young man to beg a girl whom he has known for only five weeks to marry him. She asks for time to consider, and he returns home. A year later he is shocked to receive a letter from the girl declaring that she loves him too and wants to marry him. But to him, "It was as if one loved, and dead and forgotten had returned to life; with the strange illusion that the rush of existence had halted while she lay in her grave; and with the still more singular delusion that love is eternal." But the man never considers telling her that this is a different summer and he a different soul. He goes to her, "As he would have gone unflinchingly to meet the business obligation that he knew would leave him bankrupt" (457). Thus the girl's illusion that love is eternal and the man's illusion that one should never break a commitment lead the two into a tragic union.

In "The Recovery" a blind woman recovers her sight after fifteen years of blindness, but in doing so loses an important illusion. Accustomed to living in a dark world and to thinking of herself as she looked at twenty, the woman as a result of her recovery faces a crisis.

She first sees again on a June day. "Glad almost to ecstacy, she was yet afraid" and prefers to see first "the dumb inanimate objects around her before gazing into the dear familiar faces." The sun-washed beauty of the world outside almost overwhelms her: "'The world has not changed,' she murmured; 'it has only grown more beautiful. Oh, I had forgotten how beautiful!'" (480). For a while she coyly postpones looking into the mirror, but at last she does confront her own image. The sight stuns her: "'Mother!' she cried, involuntarily, turning swiftly; but she was still alone. . . . The eyes, above all, seemed to speak to her. Afflicted as they had been, they alone belonged to that old, other self that had somewhere vanished" (481). All the beauty of the June day, seeing again the dear faces of those she loves—nothing compensates for the loss of "that old, other self."

Fickle Fate and Fickle People

Four stories deal with the fickleness of fate and of people, aspects of life that no serious observer can overlook.

"The Blind Man" shows the vagaries of fate when a streetcar strikes down a wealthy man with perfect hearing and sight instead of a poor, blind beggar with no defense against traffic hazards and nothing to lose except life itself. This story also juxtaposes the world's cold indifference toward the constant suffering of the beggar with its shocked horror at the sudden death of the rich man. In "Elizabeth Stock's One Story," the fickleness of both fortune and people conspire to rob a good woman of her job, her health, and finally her life.

In "The Kiss" Nathalie plots to marry Brantain for his wealth yet continue a torrid affair with his friend Harvy. At the wedding reception Harvy finds her alone and says, "I don't know what you've been telling [Brantain] . . . but he has sent me here to kiss you." She feels smug, and "her lips looked hungry for the kiss which they invited." But Harvy adds that he has given up kissing women: "it's dangerous" (381), he declares.

"Ti Démon" reveals the importance of both chance and a person's name in shaping his life. The protagonist is a mild person whose mother had fondly dubbed him Ti Démon when, as a crying infant, he kept her awake nights. The name sticks with him through many years of gentle behavior until finally one night his fickle fiancée and a man he thinks is his friend betray him. He becomes so angry that he actually does behave violently for the only time in his life. Thereafter, people regard him with awe and terror, saying, "he's dangerous him—they call him Ti Démon" (627). His mother's whimsy in nicknaming him, the faithlessness of those he loves, and the caprices of public opinion severely circumscribe his life.

The Power of Sex

"Ti Démon" illustrates that human fickleness, sometimes compounded by the caprices of fortune, may shape one's reputation and character. But in seven stories of this group Chopin suggests that another power—the power of sex—often exerts the strongest force in forming personality and character. In "The Unexpected" the thought of sexual contact with her fiancé— formerly handsome and well built but now wasted from illness— repels the protagonist so strongly that she gains unwelcome insights into herself. In "A Mental Suggestion" sexual love transforms the protagonist into a better person. In "Suzette," "Fedora," and "The Godmother," however, sexual feelings nudge the protagonists toward strange, unnatural, or even cruel behavior. And finally, in the title story, sexual magnetism virtually determines the protagonist's life-style, his knowledge of himself, even his name.

Cruel or perverting love.   "Suzette" explores some unpleasant aspects of infatuation. The title character is prinking before a small mirror when Ma'ma Zidore tells her that one of her suitors, Michel Jardeau, has drowned. Suzette feels sure that Michel has taken his own life because of his hopeless love for her, but she scarcely reacts at all: "her eyes . . . gleamed, but not with tears. Regret over . . . 'poor Michel' was in nowise distracting her . . . from the careful arrangement of . . . her lustrous brown hair." The young coquette idly wonders why she does not care, although a year before she had loved Michel "desperately." At that time he had "seemed to care for little Pavie Ombre"; but at a barbecue "sudden infatuation" for Suzette had seized him, and he "stayed beside her the whole day long; turning her head with his . . . soft touches. . . . after that day he cared no longer for . . . any woman . . . besides Suzette. What a weariness that love had finally become to her, only herself knew" (558). Meanwhile Pavie continues loving Michel. Upon hearing of his death, she first falls "in a white, dead faint." Then she wails and sobs, "indifferent to those who might hear her in passing along the road" (558). And nearby Suzette continues preening herself until she hears cattle approaching. Then she rushes to the window and rivets her attention on one of the cowboys driving the herd. But he does not even glance at her. "Suzette turned from the window—her face gray and pinched, with all the warmth and color gone out of it. She flung herself upon the bed and there she cried and moaned with wrenching sobs between" (559). So Suzette and Michel alike seem to want only to attract the objects of their desire physically, not to develop knowing, loving relationships with them.

Theordore Dreiser's 1918 story "The Second Choice"[7] seems patterned after "Suzette" in both characters and theme. Shirley and Arthur in Dreiser's story—like Suzette, Michel, and the cowboy in Chopin's—exhibit an appalling lack of compassion for the persons whom they attract. And Dreiser's Barton resembles Chopin's Pavie in his utter bondage to infatuation and his lack of self-respect.

The drive to know love and to satisfy it physically may shape a woman's character, whether the drive is frustrated or fulfilled. "Fedora" features a thirty-year-old spinster who has forged a place for herself among her brothers, her sisters, and their guests by assuming an elderly air of stern authority: "Fedora was tall and slim, and carried her head loftily, and wore eyeglasses and a severe expression" (467). She has for eight years known young Malthers, now a big, handsome man of twenty-three, to whom she suddenly finds herself strongly attracted: "the sudden realization came home to her that he was a man—in voice, in attitude, in bearing, in every sense—a man." From that moment "She wanted him by her, though his

nearness troubled her. There was uneasiness, restlessness, expectation
when he was not there within sight or sound. There was redoubled uneasiness when he was by—there was inward revolt, astonishment, rapture"
(467–68). But of course, young Malthers feels no such passion for Fedora;
indeed, he would surely be astonished to learn that the spinster is even
capable of such feelings.

When Malthers's sister comes to visit, Fedora announces that she will
meet the girl's train, because "the brute was restive, and shouldn't be trusted to the handling of the young people" (467). The girl, Fedora finds,
looks disturbingly like her brother, but in miniature. She sits "lower in the
cart than Fedora, who drove, handling whip and rein with accomplished
skill." Fedora, "in her usual elderly fashion," tells Miss Malthers that she
hopes the girl will come to her "freely and without reserve" with all her
wants and needs. Fedora "had gathered the reins into one hand, and with
the other free arm she encircled Miss Malthers' shoulders. When the girl
looked up into her face with murmured thanks, Fedora bent down and
pressed a long, penetrating kiss upon her mouth" (469).

Robert Arner discusses well the homosexual overtones of Fedora'a actions.[8] But he does not mention Chopin's emphasis on Fedora's lust for Mr.
Malthers nor the spinster's conflicting needs for a place where she feels that
she belongs and for sexual love. Her attitude toward the small girl who
looks like the man for whom she yearns seems to be an attempt to reconcile
these conflicting forces.[9]

"The Godmother" features a complex character named Tante Elodie who
also acts strangely and even tragically because of frustrated love, both maternal and sexual. The story opens on a cheery scene with several persons—
including Elodie's godson, Gabriel Lucaze—gathered around her glowing
fire one February evening. Tante Elodie, another spinster, dotes on Gabriel, who is the son of the man she would have married except for her
parents' intervention. Gabriel stays and plays cribbage with Tante Elodie
for a time after the others leave that evening. Then he too goes out.

But very late he returns, telling of having murdered a man in an old
deserted cabin and then having fled the scene. Tante Elodie tells him repeatedly that he did not kill anyone: "'You 'ave not killed the man Ever-
son,' she said deliberately. 'You know nothing about 'im.'" She arranges
his alibi, tidies his appearance, and sends "him away with a thousand reiterated precautions" (603). Then she goes to the cabin, rifles the dead man's
pockets to simulate a robbery, and retrieves Gabriel's knife. Consequently
no one suspects Gabriel of the crime. But he finds accepting himself as
hot-headed killer easier than accepting Tante Elodie as cold-blooded ac-

complice. He avoids her and seeks escape from his guilt feelings through wild drinking sprees. Meanwhile guilt is consuming Tante Elodie as surely as it is Gabriel, causing her health to fail and her body to waste away.

Eventually Gabriel dies in an accident, and the old woman feels only relief because now he cannot betray himself. The shriveled, lonely person Tante Elodie has become—"She stayed there alone in the corner, under the deep shadow of the oaks" (614)—contrasts vividly with the warm, attractive woman described at the beginning amid "a group of young people gathered about her fire" (597). Acting out the role of mother to the son of the man she loves does not adequately substitute for sexually expressing her love for the man or for having a son herself. She bestows all of her passion upon the godson in an unnatural relationship that leads to disaster for all concerned.

Magnetic power of sex. The title story, "A Vocation and a Voice,"[10] makes clear that Chopin knew the strength of sexual attraction. Although "many editors"[11] refused the story, written in 1896, the *St. Louis Mirror* did publish it on 27 March 1902. The story features a homeless, loveless, even nameless protagonist who is called only "the boy" until almost the end of the narrative. "A Vocation and a Voice" essentially tells the story of the boy's search for his own identity, for his answer to Lear's question, "Who am I?"

Mrs. Donnelly, with whose family the boy lives as "an alien member" in "The Patch," has sent him on an errand to a distant part of the city; as he makes his way on foot back toward "The Patch," he progresses slowly because "With him was a conviction that it would make no difference to any one whether he got back to 'The Patch' or not." Having "a vague sense of being unessential which always dwelt with him" (521), the boy haphazardly goes along with a gypsy couple he encounters. He enjoys camping out and contributes his share to the group's welfare by doing various chores.

By calling him only "the boy," the narrator emphasizes his youthful innocence: "He was rather tall, though he had spoken with the high, treble voice of a girl" (520). Further, "The young girls did not attract him more than the boys or the little children" (522). As the story unfolds, his namelessness poignantly emphasizes the universality of his experiences—the loss of innocence and the accompanying search for place, love, and knowledge of self.

Suzima, the female half of the nomadic couple he joins, appears "robust and young—twenty or thereabouts—and comely, in a certain rude, vigorous fashion" (523). When the boy happens along, she is beating out a grass

fire while cursing her absent husband, who makes a habit of getting drunk
whenever camp-breaking time arrives. She says, "I guess he's drunk down
there—him and his mules! He thinks more of them mules than he does of
me and the whole world put together"(525).

The husband, Gutro, returns. He is "a short, broad-girted man. . . .
His hair, as well as his beard, was long, curly and greasy; . . . he wore a
slouch felt hat over a knotted red handkerchief and small golden hoops in
his ears" (525). The narrator often calls him simply "the Beast."

The boy finds a place, of sorts, with this make-shift family as they make
their leisurely way southward. "The days were a gorgeous, golden proces-
sional, good and warm with sunshine, and languorous" (526). They stop
for a month near a village, where the boy renews his close contact with the
Catholic church. When Suzima and Gutro decide to move on at the end of
a month, the village priest tries to get the boy to stay. But the boy refuses:
"'I got to go,' he murmured. . . . Yes, he wanted to lead an up-right,
clean existence before God and man. . . . He liked the village, the people,
the life which he had led there. Above all he liked the man whose kindly
spirit had been moved to speak and act in his behalf. But the stars were
beginning to shine and he thought of the still nights in the forest. A savage
instinct stirred within him" (536). Perhaps the man is beginning to awak-
en within the boy.

Suzima often sings as the three walk along the road. "The boy thought
he had never heard anything more beautiful than the full, free notes that
came from her throat, filling the vast, woody temple with melody. It was
always the same stately refrain from some remembered opera that she sang"
(527). In fact, "the one stately refrain" (533) grows so familiar to the boy
that he sometimes hears it in his dreams.

This idyllic existence continues until one day the boy happens upon
Suzima bathing nude in a little stream. "He saw her as one sees an object
in a flash from a dark sky—sharply, vividly. Her image, against the background of tender green, ate into his brain and into his flesh with the fixed-
ness and intensity of white-hot iron." Afterward the woman at first acts
"less kind" (539) to him, but they soon become lovers.

The sexual experience produces an immediate, dramatic effect: "A few
days had wrought great changes with the boy. That which he had known
before he now comprehended, and with comprehension sympathy awoke.
He seemed to have been brought in touch with the universe of men and all
things that live. He cared more than ever for the creeping and crawling
things, for the beautiful voiceless life that met him at every turn; . . . that
silently unfolded the mysterious, inevitable existence" (541). Thus the boy

who began the story without place, love, or knowledge of himself has found all three.

But inevitably his love for Suzima and his new comprehension of life soon make his place as "the boy" in this household untenable. A quarrel between Gutro and Suzima sets off the explosion: "Suddenly, the man, in a rage, turned to strike her with a halter that he held uplifted, but, quicker than he, the boy was ready with a pointed hunting knife that he seized from the ground" (542). Although the fracas causes no serious physical injuries, its results nevertheless reach far.

The boy thus encounters an abrupt challenge not only to his delicious new feeling of understanding and sympathy with all of life but even to his long-held concept of his own inner person: "He had always supposed that he could live in the world a blameless life. . . . He had never dreamed of a devil lurking unknown to him, in his blood, that would some day blind him, disable his will and direct his hands to deeds of violence. . . . He felt as if he had encountered some hideous being with whom he was not acquainted and who had said to him: 'I am yourself'" (542). This new concept of himself he finds unbearable, and so he enters a monastery, the "Refuge" (544), where he succeeds for years in hiding from the "devil lurking . . . in his blood."

At the Refuge the boy acquires a new sense of who he is and, at last, even a name—Brother Ludovic: "He often felt that he had been born anew, the day whereupon he had entered the gate of this holy refuge. That hideous, evil spectre of himself lurking outside, ready at any moment to claim him should he venture within its reach, was, for a long time, a menace to him. But he had come to dread it no longer, secure in the promise of peace which his present life held out to him" (543–44). Thus he comes to feel secure in his new place and in his knowledge of himself.

Brother Ludovic has a great dream, to build a solid stone wall around the Refuge. He works feverishly at this task that will take a lifetime to complete. "He liked to picture himself an old man, grown feeble with age, living upon this peaceful summit all enclosed by the solid stone wall built with the strength of his youth and manhood" (544).

But he learns that this self-image, too, lacks completeness. One day while working on his wall, "Suddenly Brother Ludovic stopped, lifting his head with the mute quivering attention of some animal in the forest, startled at the scent of approaching danger. . . . The air was hot and heavy. . . . He could hear soft splashing at the pool. An image that had once been branded into his soul . . . unfolded before his vision with the poignancy of life" (545). These strong appeals to the senses of smell, sight,

hearing, and touch remind the reader that Brother Ludovic remains a physical being as well as a spiritual one. Then a distant sound draws nearer, and
the images grow more sensual: "He had heard the voice of a woman sing-
ing the catchy refrain from an opera. . . . The sound was faint and distant,
but it was approaching, coming nearer and nearer." Finally, the sexual
magnetism overwhelms Brother Ludovic: "He was conscious of nothing in
the world but the voice that was calling him and the cry of his own being
that responded. Brother Ludovic bounded down from the wall and followed the voice of the woman" (546). Thus Brother Ludovic learns that he
needs more from life than a secure place, even the "Refuge"; that nothing,
not even rock walls, will contain the force of sexual attraction; and that he
may never know fully that complex person who dwells within himself.

Despite the distinctly masculine point of view in "A Vocation and a
Voice," the boy exhibits universal, conflicting needs that transcend the
limitations of gender. In Chopin's day society allowed, although it did not
encourage, a writer to examine these human needs from the masculine
point of view. But when the same author later offered in *The Awakening* a
female character, Edna Pontellier, engaged in a similar struggle to find
herself, the public and most literary critics ostracized Chopin and her
works, bringing to a virtual conclusion her literary career.

"Free! Body and soul free!" "The Story of an Hour" Per Seyersted
calls Chopin's "most startling picture of female self-assertion."[12] In it Mrs.
Mallard, a lady with a weak heart, learns that her husband has been killed.
She weeps "with sudden, wild abandonment"; and when "the storm of
grief had spent itself" (352), she goes to her room alone, where she sits for
a time encased in her grief. The lines of Mrs. Mallard's "fair, calm face . . .
bespoke repression." She feels something approaching her, something almost tangible:

There was something coming to her. . . . What was it? She did not know. . . .
But she felt it . . . reaching toward her through the sounds, the scents, the color
that filled the air.
    . . . She was beginning to recognize this thing that was approaching to possess
her, and she was striving to beat it back with her will. . . .
    When she abandoned herself a little whispered word escaped her. . . . She said
it over and over under her breath: "free, free, free!" (353)

Mrs. Mallard knows that she will cry again for the loss of a kind, loving
husband. She clearly has had the first two of those three qualities—love,

place, and autonomy—which Chopin associates with the full life. But the narrator exclaims:

What did it matter! What could love, the unsolved mystery, count for in face of this possession of self-assertion which she suddenly recognized as the strongest impulse of her being!
"Free! Body and soul free!" she kept whispering. (353–54)

The stories Chopin wanted to include in this volume do indeed bring her characters into clear focus, and some of these characters refuse to settle quietly for lives of only partial fulfillment. Mrs. Mallard, for example, discovers that no amount of love and security can compensate for a lack of control over her own existence.

Chapter Six
Miscellaneous Works

In addition to the collected stories already discussed and two novels to be examined later, Chopin wrote twenty-nine complete stories or sketches, an insignificant one-act play, forty-six poems, and thirteen essays about literature. The uncollected stories include several beginner's sketches but also some of her best short fiction. Although lacking excellence, a few of the poems confirm themes observed in her stories. And most of the essays express effectively ideas consistent with those in her fiction; further, one or two provide a glimpse into Chopin's own person, an entity she usually takes care to keep private.

Uncollected Stories

Looking at Chopin's uncollected stories in the order written offers an overview of her entire career from its first gropings (1889–93), through its powerful maturity (1894–98), and finally into the anticlimactic return to its beginnings (1899–1903). The work of her best years shows that she achieved remarkable craftsmanship quickly. But the subject matter remains consistent throughout, with her primary concern usually being the conflicting nature of people's needs for a secure place or role in life, for love, and for autonomy.

"Emancipation": The constant theme. When only about eighteen years old, before she married and twenty years before she evinced any interest in a literary career, Kate O'Flaherty wrote a little sketch entitled "Emancipation: A Life Fable" in which she spells out the theme that permeates her fiction. Her life and experiences as a woman apparently affirmed the truths she expressed first in "Emancipation," and her development as a literary artist enabled her to transpose those truths into art with increasing skill until at last *The Awakening,* the fully artistic expression of her theme, became possible.

The 1869 or 1870 "Fable" describes an animal "born in a cage," who "opening his eyes upon Life . . . saw . . . confining walls." He thrives until one day someone accidentally leaves open the cage's door. He first reacts with fear, but the "Light" lures him with increasing force until at last the "spell of the Unknown" pulls him out altogether, "and with a bound he was gone" (37).

No longer protected by the cage, "On he rushes, . . . wounding and tearing his sleek sides, seeing, smelling, touching of all things." Gone is the "invisible protecting hand," and the animal discovers that "hungering there is no food but such as he must seek and ofttimes fight for; and his limbs are weighted before he reaches the water that is good to his thirsting throat." He could return to the cage, but he does not: "So does he live, seeking, finding, joying and suffering. The door which accident had opened is open still, but the cage remains forever empty" (37–38). The animal, rejecting security within the cage, embraces life with all its suffering and sorrows.

Seyersted suggests that the eighteen-year-old Kate, probably having recently met Oscar Chopin, is expressing a desire to escape the "childhood cage."[1] Her age and circumstances at the time lend credence to such an interpretation. Another possible reading grows from the similarity between the "cage" and the Garden of Eden, described in Genesis 2:8–25, with the "animal" like Adam and Eve choosing to eat from the "tree of life" rather than to live forever protected in paradise. In any case, the stories already examined make clear that Chopin felt special compassion for anyone trapped by circumstances such as childhood, poverty, race, or sex. And if one looks back upon "Emancipation" after reading "The Story of an Hour," "Her Letters," "Athénaïse," and especially *The Awakening,* the cared-for animal seems startlingly similar to the cared-for woman of the later stories.

In his cage he lives "under care of an invisible protecting hand. Hungering, food was ever at hand. When he thirsted water was brought; . . . he found it good, licking his handsome flanks, to bask in the sun" (37). Clearly he has no more reason to wish to escape his cage and his kind, generous keeper than Edna Pontellier will have almost thirty years later to desert her home and her kind, generous husband. If they had remained in their respective places of security, both the animal and Edna could have escaped much pain, but they could never have explored their worlds or their souls.

A beginner's efforts: 1889–93. In June 1889, twenty years after "Emancipation," Chopin first wrote a story that was published. The title, "Wiser than a God," comes from the Latin proverb "To love and be wise is scarcely granted even to a god" (39). Its protagonist, Paula Von Stoltz, falls in love with George Brainard, and he with her. Dedicated to becoming a

great pianist, Paula has learned to sacrifice everything for her art. But
George, whom she loves passionately, has every quality a girl could hope
for in a husband: he is handsome, wealthy, kind, considerate, and intelligent. Further he does not ask Paula to give up her music or her ambitions.
Yet Paula, being "wiser than a god," apparently realizes that she cannot be
both Paula Von Stoltz, a great musician, and Mrs. George Brainard. She
chooses to remain the former, but doing so requires her to sacrifice love.

Two months after "Wiser than a God," Chopin wrote "A Point at Issue," another story featuring a strong woman. Its heroine, Eleanor Gail,
values "free thought" and "spiritual emancipation" (48). Charles Faraday,
a young mathematics professor, thinks her the ideal woman, graced with
both "womanly charms" and a "logical" mind (49). They marry, agreeing
that their marriage shall not "touch the individuality of either." For Elean-
or, "marriage, which marks too often the closing period of a woman's intellectual existence, was to be . . . the open portal through which she
might seek the embellishments that her strong, graceful mentality deserved" (50).

Because Eleanor wants to learn French, she resides in Paris while Charles
remains in America, and both experience jealousy during the long separa-
tion. But when Charles learns of Eleanor's irrational feelings, he thinks,
"my Nellie is only a woman, after all," quite forgetting his own jealousy.
They decide that their love must after all take priority over Eleanor's "intellectual existence," and so she returns to America with Charles.

Thus Chopin's first two published stories develop the same theme: a
married woman cannot maintain her own individuality. Eleanor Gail must
either remain Eleanor Gail or become Mrs. Charles Faraday. She cannot be
both, as she attempts to be, even though much of her attraction to Charles
results from "the beautiful revelations of her mind" (49). Although he believes as strongly as she that after their marriage each should "remain a free
integral of humanity" (50), Charles nevertheless fairly smirks as he thinks,
"my Nellie is only woman after all." And of course it is Nellie who gives
up her ambitions and returns to America so that the couple can be
together.

In November and December 1889, Chopin wrote two little tales for the
popular magazines. One, "Miss Witherwell's Mistake," tells of a young
couple who employ a gentle ruse to overcome parental objections to their
marriage. The other, "With the Violin," relates a Christmas story featuring
miraculous blessings and angelic music.

Chopin wrote the next story not included in her collections, "Mrs.
Mobry's Reason," on 10 January 1891. Its protagonist, Editha Payne, re-

fuses for three years to marry John Mobry, the man she loves. But at last she becomes his wife, and in due time they have a son and a daughter, Edward and Naomi. Despite Mrs. Mobry's intense efforts to prevent his doing so, Edward eventually marries and fathers a child. The mother likewise attempts to prevent Naomi from falling in love. At last Mrs. Mobry's "reason" becomes apparent when Naomi becomes mentally deranged. Editha cries to her husband with "terror in her eyes": "Oh, God! if it might end with me and with her—my stricken dove! But . . . Edward has already a child. Others will be born to him, and I see the crime of my marriage reaching out to curse me though the lips of generations that will come" (79). Susan Wolstenholme believes that this story shows the influence of Ibsen,[2] notwithstanding Chopin's own statement that "Ibsen will not be true . . . to-morrow" because of his penchant for treating "mutable" social problems (693). Certainly "Mrs. Mobry's Reason" indicates that the theories of biological determinism influenced Chopin and perhaps that the biblical idea of the punishment for sins extending to future generations concerned her too.

"The Going Away of Liza," written 4 April 1891, features Chopin's first protagonist who leaves her husband.[3] Liza leaves good, kind Abner because she "craves to taste the joys of ixistence [*sic*]" (113). Eventually, however, hunger forces her to return, and "of all the voices that clamored in [Abner's] soul . . . that of the outraged husband was the loudest" (114). At his mother's prodding, however, his natural kindness prevails and, kneeling at Liza's feet, he removes her wet, tattered shoes. The clash between Liza's drive "to taste the joys of ixistence" and Abner's need to act "the outraged husband" lifts this maudlin story above its otherwise incredible sentimentality.

"The Maid of St. Phillippe," written the same month as "The Going Away of Liza," is even weaker; but its protagonist, Marianne, also longs for freedom. She refuses to marry, declaring: "I have breathed the free air. . . . I was not born to be the mother of slaves." The young man demands: "What do you mean, Marianne? . . . what is left for you?" And she exclaims, "Freedom is left for me!" (122).

Two months later Chopin wrote "A Shameful Affair," a much better story. Mildred Orme, another strong heroine, is slightly attracted to a hand on a farm where she is visiting. Bored, she openly flirts with him. He repulses her rudely, thus increasing her interest. She follows him to the river one day, whereupon he kisses her passionately. Shocked at her own pleasure, she nevertheless refuses to avoid seeing the man during subsequent days. One day he apologizes and asks her forgiveness. She replies enigmatically, "Some day—perhaps; when I shall have forgiven myself" (136). Though shallow and spoiled, Mildred confronts herself and others directly; she violates conventional rules of conduct by throwing herself at a man (and one far below her in status, at that), by enjoying the kiss that "rifled" her "chaste lips" of "their innocence" (134), by refusing to avoid seeing him after he has shamed her, by admitting to herself that she enjoyed the kiss, and most of all by admitting as much to him also. She is well on the way to becoming an autonomous individual.

In September 1891 Chopin wrote two more stories that foreshadow later, better works. "A Harbinger" (11 September 1891), although only a sketch, resembles "A Shameful Affair" in dealing with a woman's awakening interest in sex. And "Doctor Chevalier's Lie," said by Rankin to be the account of "an actual incident in the life of a physician of New Orleans,"[4] relates the commonplace story of a country girl corrupted by the evil city. But Chopin stresses the girl's misfortune rather than her moral corruption. This nameless girl had simply gone "to seek her fortune in the city" (147); but she, like many other Chopin heroines who seek their own "fortunes" or even the opportunity to develop into discrete individuals, goes down to defeat in her search.

The uncollected stories of 1892 begin with a couple of children's tales, "Croque-Mitaine" (27 February 1892) and "A Little Free-Mulatto" (28 February 1892). And finally, "Miss McEnders" (7 March 1892) incorporates some social satire, a rare element in Chopin's fiction. Seyersted makes the interesting point that Chopin, original as usual, directs her sarcasm against the "do-gooder," not the corrupt businessman in the story.[5]

The mature artist: 1894–98.   As Chopin's skills developed, she collected more of her stories in the volumes for publication; the next uncollected story, "Vagabonds," was not written until probably December 1895, almost four years after "Miss McEnders."

This story is one of several in which Chopin expresses envy for the carefree life of the tramp. The individual without home, job, or apparent family ties may be assumed to have little love or sense of belonging; but he does very nearly achieve autonomy, and Chopin may have longed for such control over her own life, even though she clearly enjoyed her family ties.

Perhaps because "Vagabonds" describes an incident from her own life,[6] she departs from her characteristic third-person point of view to use a first-person narrator, who says of the tramp, "I could not help thinking that it must be good to prowl sometimes; to get close to the black night and lose oneself in its silence and mystery" (472). So in "Vagabonds" the character loses himself in the "mystery" of the night; three years later in *The Awak-*

ening, Edna will be "seeking herself and finding herself" in "the mystery" (934) of a similar night. Thus the night would seem to be linked in Chopin's thought with the self—both being deep, mysterious, unfathomable, fascinating.

"Madame Martel's Christmas Eve," written in January 1896, tells of a widow who makes "a luxury of grief." Although her husband has been dead for six years, she continues her mourning and "never intended to lay it aside" (474). Her friends and children almost revere her fidelity, but they do not enjoy being with her, especially on happy occasions; and the story implies that a woman should have a more satisfying place in life than mere widowhood can provide.

Madame Martel's adjustment to widowhood may resemble that of Kate O'Flaherty's mother, whose home never lost its air of sadness after her husband's death, according to Rankin.[7] And Seyersted suggests that Madame Martel resembles also Kate Chopin because the widowed author was reluctant to remarry for fear that she could not be as close with anyone else as she had been with Oscar.[8] But Chopin does not seem to have spent her years after Oscar's death hiding behind a widow's veils. Indeed, almost two years before writing this story, Chopin mused in her diary: "If it were possible for my husband and my mother to come back to earth, I feel that I would unhesitatingly give up every thing that has come into my life since they left it and join my existence again with theirs. To do that, I would have to forget the past ten years of my growth—my real growth."[9] Whereas Madame Martel has spent her six years of widowhood trying to avoid making her own acquaintance and attempting to hang onto her former identity, Chopin speaks of "emerging [in about 1888] from the vast solitude in which I had been making my own acquaintance" (700). Thus an autobiographical interpretation of Madame Martel seems inconsistent with Chopin's account of her own experience.

Also written in early 1896, "A Pair of Silk Stockings" tells the story of another widow, the poverty-stricken Mrs. Sommers, who unexpectedly receives fifteen dollars. She dreams of outfitting her four children in new clothes: "The vision of her little brood looking fresh and dainty and new for once in their lives excited her" (500). Mrs. Sommers seems at first to be one of the type of women later described in *The Awakening* as "mother-women," those "who idolized their children . . . and esteemed it a holy privilege to efface themselves" (888). But Mrs. Sommers goes out and spends the entire sum on personal luxuries for herself: a pair of silk stockings—"How good was the touch of raw silk to her flesh!" (502); stylish boots; luxurious gloves; two expensive magazines, "such as she had been accustomed to read in the days when she had been accustomed to other pleasant things" (503); lunch in a fine restaurant; and a matinee theatrical performance.

But then, of course, "The play was over, the music ceased, the crowd filed out. It was like a dream ended. . . . Mrs. Sommers went to the corner and waited for the cable car." Now she must return to the "real" world and to her "real" identity, that of the "mother-woman." But she goes with a "powerful longing that the cable car would never stop anywhere, but go on and on with her forever" (504). No hint of censure for her selfishness colors the picture of this young mother. Indeed, the reader feels deep compassion for her.

In "Aunt Lympy's Interference," written in June 1896, Melitte earns her living teaching school. Her father had once owned a prosperous plantation, and one of his former slaves is Aunt Lympy—another of Chopin's caste-conscious black people like Chicot in "Nég Créol," Uncle Oswald in "The Bênitous' Slave," and Tante Cat'rinette in the story of the same name. Aunt Lympy learns of Melitte's "shame" (513) and "interferes," with the net result that Melitte gets married and stops teaching, thus moving into a more appropriate social position, at least in Aunt Lympy's opinion.

In March 1897 Chopin wrote "The Locket," an insignificant story in which a scared, young soldier steals a locket, apparently thinking it is a lucky charm; but he cannot fool the fates and loses his life anyway. "A Family Affair," also written in 1897, presents a memorable portrait of Madame Solisainte, an enormously fat, selfish, repulsive woman. Growing too old and obese to walk but being too miserly to hire someone to care for her, she decides to have a niece named Bosey come to live with her. Through the sheer force of her character, Bosey assumes full authority, buying the supplies and medical attention her aunt needs while the stingy old woman stews helplessly. The girl eventually announces that she plans to marry and go away. But she has one last surprise in store for her aunt, who had taken possession of all the family heirlooms years earlier when her mother, Bosey's grandmother, died. Before leaving, Bosey says off-handedly: "by the way, *Tante* Félicie, . . . I have made an equal division of grandmother's silver and table linen and jewels which I found in the strong box, and sent them to mamma. You know yourself it was only just; mamma had as much right to them as you. So, good-by, *Tante* Félicie. You are quite sure you wouldn't like to have Sister Adèle?" (583–84). Enraged, the old woman staggers to her feet and gropes her way to her treasure room without help from anyone. As Robert Arner suggests, a few years earlier Chopin might have ended the story sentimentally with a reconciliation effected through Madame Solisainte's miraculous cure. [10] But by December 1897, when she probably wrote "A Family Affair," Chopin realized that an honest character portrayal must respect the strong human tendency toward continuity. Therefore, she closes with a highly dramatic word picture of the gross old woman tottering along and shouting, "I will 'ave the law! . . . I will 'ave the law!" (585).

Early in the summer of 1898 publishers accepted both *The Awakening* and the collection "A Vocation and a Voice." These acceptances apparently emboldened Chopin, for on 18 or 19 July [11] she wrote "The Storm," one of the most daring stories in American literature to that time. She subtitled it "A Sequel to 'At the 'Cadian Ball'": just as the earlier story turns upon the passionate interest between Alcée and Calixta that had first flamed a year before the story itself begins, so "The Storm" also pivots upon that same body chemistry. Although Calixta and Alcée apparently have not seen each other since that night at the ball six years before, the sexual magnetism between them still pulses as strongly as ever.

The story opens with Bobinôt and Bibi, Calixta's husband and four-year-old son, caught at the store by a sudden storm. Afraid that the tempest will frighten Calixta, Bobinôt buys her some shrimps to make up for having left her alone.

The scene now shifts to Calixta at home. Alcée Laballière rides in at the gate and asks if he may wait on Calixta's gallery until the rain passes over. Almost immediately, however, the wind and rain force him to seek better shelter inside. Calixta, frightened by a lightning bolt, staggers backward into Alcée's arms. At the touch of their bodies, the strong passion that had charged the atmosphere leaps all bounds. Alcée murmurs hoarsely:

"Do you remember—in Assumption, Calixta?" . . . Oh! she remembered; for in Assumption he had kissed her and kissed and kissed her; until his senses would well nigh fail, and to save her he would resort to a desperate flight. If she was not an immaculate dove in those days, she was still inviolate; a passionate creature whose very defenselessness had made her defense, against which his honor forbade him to prevail. Now—well, now—her lips seemed in a manner free to be tasted, as well as her round, white throat and her whiter breasts. (594)

The course of their passion parallels that of the storm until at last "they seemed to swoon together at the very borderland of life's mystery." The thunder recedes; the rain stops; Alcée rides away; Calixta "lifted her pretty chin in the air and laughed aloud" (595).

Bobinôt and Bibi come home, where Calixta greets them with warm affection and good humor. Alcée writes lovingly to Clarisse, telling her to remain with the babies at Biloxi another month if she wishes. Clarisse receives the letter with pleasure, because her "first free breath since her marriage" has made her feel again the "pleasant liberty of her maiden days" and, "devoted as she was to her husband, their intimate conjugal life was something which she was more than willing to forego for a while" (596). So the storm leaves everyone happy. Yet the reader doubts that Alcée plans to forgo sex while Clarisse remains away, and this suspicion adds a powerful tension to the story.

Although few stories surpass "The Storm" in craftsmanship or narrative force, the angry reception given *The Awakening* early the next year prevented Chopin from even attempting to publish the story. Had she published it, no doubt the critics would have found it shocking indeed—shocking in the explicit, albeit artistic, description of the love scene; even more shocking in the fact that Calixta frankly enjoys this adulterous interlude. But the last line would probably have shocked the nineteenth-century reader more than any other part of the story: "So the storm passed and every one was happy" (596). The fact that no one pays for the sin would probably have offended the critics most of all, for even today some readers find that conclusion unforgivable.

Anticlimax: 1899–1903.   After "The Storm" Chopin seems to have written no fiction except an unimportant children's story, "A Little Country Girl," and the previously discussed "The Godmother" until after *The Awakening* appeared on 22 April 1899. Apparently she was waiting to learn how critics and the public would receive her mildly daring new novel. The answer came quickly. Less that two weeks after the novel's release, Frances Porcher's review in the *St. Louis Mirror* (4 May 1899) set the pattern of general condemnation, thus extinguishing Chopin's hopes that she might be able to publish the far more daring "The Storm" and perhaps other similarly bold stories yet unwritten. In February 1900 Herbert S. Stone & Co. returned without explanation her previously accepted collection "A Vocation and a Voice." The publisher may well have had reasons unrelated to the controversy surrounding *The Awakening,* but Chopin took the lack of explanation as another indication that her literary career had ended.[12]

She apparently wrote only two brief poems from April, when the book came out, until November, when she wrote a little sketch entitled "A Reflection." In it the first-person narrator says that some people "do not need to apprehend the significance of things. They do not . . . sink by the wayside to be left contemplating the moving procession." The narrator laments not being one of those "fortunate beings" who form part of the "moving procession": "Its fantastic colors are more brilliant and beautiful than the sun on the undulating waters. What matter if souls and bodies are falling beneath the feet of the ever-pressing multitude!" That "moving procession of human energy" is "greater than the stars. . . . Oh! I could weep at being left by the wayside." But, the persona says, consolation comes because "In the procession I should feel the crushing feet, the clashing discords, the ruthless hands and stifling breath. I could not hear the rhythm of the march." And so the narrator resigns herself, saying, "Let us be still and wait by the roadside" (622). Seyersted believes that the "crushing feet" and the "stifling breath" belong to the "critics who refused to see 'the significance of things,'" thus killing Chopin's creativity.[13]

Nevertheless Chopin did try to return to "the procession" by again writing local-color stories of the *Bayou Folk* sort; but even as one can never regain lost innocence, so a writer who has explored the depths can hardly return to a surface appraisal of life. During the remaining five years of her life, Chopin apparently wrote only eight complete stories, and none of them has much significance.

In November 1899, at about the same time that she wrote "A Reflection," Chopin wrote "Ti Démon," a local-color story discussed in chapter 4, which has more in common with the 1893 story "A Gentleman of Bayou Têche," for instance, than with "The Storm" or *The Awakening*. "A December Day in Dixie," merely describing a beautiful snow-covered cotton field near Natchitoches, Louisiana, followed in January 1900. "The Gentleman from New Orleans," another local-color story written the next month and featuring Mr. and Mrs. Buddy Bénoîte, offers a bit more substance. Mr. Buddie is "a little too stout and blustering"; his wife, on the other hand, is "too faded for her years" and shows "a certain lack of self assertion which her husband regarded as the perfection of womanliness" (631). Because of her husband's possessiveness, Mrs. Buddie has not seen her parents during the several years of her marriage. The plot involves only a sentimental reversal of this situation, with Mr. Buddie, like several of Chopin's early characters, undergoing an unlikely change of personality. But Mr. Buddie's possessiveness and his opinion of what constitutes "the perfection of womanliness" align him with some of Chopin's more memorable characters, including Bud Aiken of "In Sabine" and Léonce Pontellier of *The Awakening*.

Not even Chopin's earliest stories surpass in sentimentality "Charlie," written two months after "The Gentleman from New Orleans." In it a girl grows up, falls in love, loses the man to her sister, and dedicates the rest of her life to helping her father.[14] During the next month, May 1900, Chopin wrote "The White Eagle," which according to her final list she proposed to include in "A Vocation and a Voice"; and from May 1900 until October 1901 she apparently wrote only one or two short poems. In the latter month she wrote "The Woodchoppers," developing the point that women need men to supply them with firewood. Her last two stories, "Polly" (January 1902) and "The Impossible Miss Meadows" (1903?), resemble "The Woodchoppers" in their weak superficiality. Thus Chopin's career as a writer of fiction ended almost where it had begun only a bit more than a decade—but what a decade!—before.

Poems

Although fiction provided a better medium, Chopin apparently took her efforts in verse seriously, submitting poems for publication to several different periodicals. In fact, her first published work was the poem "If It Might Be," which appeared in *America* on 10 January 1889. Most of her efforts to publish the poems met with little success, however. Seyersted included twenty poems in *The Complete Works* in 1969 and the remaining twenty-six in *A Kate Chopin Miscellany* in 1979. All but five of the forty-six poems employ the "I" persona for an intensely personal point of view, and this fact, coupled with the nature of the content, indicates that Chopin usually speaks in her own voice in her verse. Considering how carefully she conceals herself in her fiction, this apparent willingness to expose her emotions in verse is surprising.

Songs of love.   Love is the subject of most of the poems. The earliest, "If It Might Be," expresses the persona's willingness to make loving "thee" her "life's fond work" (727). "Psyche's Lament," probably written the following year, expresses longing for a lover's return. Psyche cries: "O, sombre sweetness; black-enfolden charms, / . . . / O Love, O God, O Night come back to me!" (727). "The Song Everlasting" (1893) suggests the title and theme of *The Awakening* in its two-word refrain, "Awake, Love!" (728). "You and I," written in 1893, asks: "Was it love did we feel? was it life did we live?" (728); but it offers no answers—only questions. Another 1893 poem declares that a little more health or a little more wealth is only "A boon to scatter!" But a little more or less of love, "It matters all!" (729). Still another 1893 poem describes the persona's dreams of her lover, "dreams throughout the night" (729). In "Good Night," undated but published on 22 July 1894 in the *New Orleans Times-Democrat,* the speaker declares that until her lover returns "No day will break, for me no sun will rise—/ My own, my well-beloved—good night, good night!" (730).

The sensual imagery, akin to that in her 1894 story "A Respectable Woman," makes "If Some Day" (16 August 1895) better than most of Chopin's poems. The persona longs to look into her lover's eyes "with casual, wanton glance" and "To rest my finger tips upon thy sleeve, / Or, grown more bold, upon thy swarthy cheek." The poem concludes: "I would convey to thee some faintest gleam / Of what I dare not look, or speak, or dream!" (730).

Occasional and other verses. Eight poems are addressed to individual persons on specific occasions and bear no clear relationship to the rest of her work. "Let the Night Go," a New Year's poem dated 1 January 1897, declares that the persona has "kept one little hour from the past: / A pretty thing—a bauble to hold fast" (732). "There's Music Enough" (1898) expresses the persona's sensuous pleasure in life "When the world is green and the month is May" (732). And March has its own magic, as described in "An Ecstasy of Madness" (1898):

> There's an ecstasy of madness
> Where the March Hares dwell;
> A delirium of gladness
> Too wild to tell.
>
> (732)

"Lines Suggested by Omar," "Life," and "Because—" express more philosophical ideas. For example, in "Lines Suggested by Omar," the persona declares: "I wanted God. In heaven and earth I sought, / And lo! I found him in my inmost thought" (733). The six-line "Life" (1899) expresses the persona's, and probably Chopin's, unwillingness to claim that she has discovered any final truths or moral absolutes. Probably written in 1899, "Because—" tempers the determinism Chopin sometimes espouses, as in "Two Portraits." In "Because" she says that the rest of creation functions "Because it must—"; but man, "knowing good from ill, / Chooses because he will—" (734).

Chopin wrote "The Haunted Chamber," the longest and best of her poems, at about the time she was reading proofs for *The Awakening*; and the poem presents a woman who makes the reader think of Edna. It describes a couple spending a companionable evening with bottle, cigars, and story swapping. With them, "'twas more of a joke / Than a matter of sin or a matter of shame / That a woman had fallen, and nothing to blame"

(733–34). But after the companion leaves, the haunting voice of the woman invades the persona's consciousness:

> It rose from the depths of some infinite gloom
> And its tremulous anguish filled the room.
> . . . .
> So now I must listen the whole night through
> To the torment with which I had nothing to do.
>
> (734)

Whether or not this poem represents an effort to escape autobiographical identification with her best-known protagonist,[15] it does suggest that Chopin had already formulated a "defense" for her role as Edna's creator even before the book appeared. *Book News* published that "defense" in the form of a prose essay in July after *The Awakening* came out in April. In it Chopin explains: "Having a group of people at my disposal, I thought it might be entertaining (to myself) to throw them together and see what would happen. I never dreamed of Mrs. Pontellier making such a mess of things and working out her own damnation as she did."[16] Thus the novelist, like the persona in "The Haunted Chamber," disclaims responsibility for the lack of morality in the fictional woman.

Chopin addressed what was probably the last of her poems to her childhood friend, Kitty Garesché, who entered a convent about the same time that Kate O'Flaherty married Oscar Chopin. "To the Friend of My Youth: To Kitty" expresses an undiminished affection in 1900 for her dearest friend of the 1860s (735).

In summary, then, Chopin's poetry only rarely illuminates her fictional characters or themes, but it does substantiate the conclusion gained from her stories that she attaches great importance to love, one of the three deep human needs she treats throughout her fiction.

Essays of Literary Criticism

In thirteen essays Chopin expresses sensitive, intelligent, informed opinions about literature, making clear that she took the art of writing seriously. Further, the essays provide an occasional glimpse into her inner self, which in most other contexts she carefully protects from scrutiny.

The proper province of literature. In "The Western Association of Writers" (1894), Chopin criticizes the provincialism of the members of the Western Association, making clear that she aspires to create more than local color in her own writing. She declares: "There is a very, very big world lying not wholly in northern Indiana. . . . It is human existence in its subtle, complex, true meaning, stripped of the veil with which ethical and conventional standards have draped it." Further, she charges these Western writers with naïveté, describing Spring Fountain Park, where the association usually held its annual meeting, as "a veritable garden of Eden in which the disturbing fruit of the tree of knowledge still hangs unplucked." She adds, "There is no doubt in their souls, no unrest" (691).

In a 6 October 1894 review of *Crumbling Idols* for *St. Louis Life*, Chopin takes Hamlin Garland to task for his opinion that "social problems, social environments, local color . . . are *of themselves* motives to insure the survival of a writer." Agreeing with Garland that "conventionalism" exerts an unfortuanate influence upon young artists, she nevertheless believes that "Mr. Garland undervalues the importance of the past in art and exaggerates the significance of the present" (693). Elaborating on the mutable qualities of social problems and the immutable qualities of human nature, she continues: "Human impulses do not change and can not so long as men and women continue to stand in the relation to one another which they have occupied since our knowledge of their existence began. It is why Aeschylus is true, and Shakespeare is true to-day, and why Ibsen will not be true in some remote to-morrow, . . . because he takes for his themes social problems which by their very nature are mutable" (693). Chopin, then, believes that the male-female relationship lies among the immutable realities. How a woman like Edna Pontellier struggles in learning the terms of that reality or in futilely attempting to change those terms makes an interesting study. But, Chopin implies, only the most arrogant of writters would think that they could through the influence of their art change something so immutable as the "relation to each other" in which men and women stand.

Further, she suggests what she believes to be appropriate subject matter for a writer: "The author of 'Crumbling Idols' would even lightly dismiss from the artist's consideration such primitive passions as love, hate, etc. He declares that in real life people do not talk love. How does he know? I feel very sorry for Mr. Garland" (693–94). Chopin, for her part, constantly treats the human passions, especially love, in her art. Ultimately, whatever happens inside the emotional center of the individual Chopin sees as proper subject matter for literature, and nothing interests her more than an individual's attempts to come to terms with his or her own emotional center.

The "real" and the "true." The publication, under the title "The Real Edwin Booth," of certain private letters written by the late actor provoked Chopin to present an article under the same title in *St. Louis Life* on 13 October 1894. Empathetic with Booth's "mantle of sensitiveness and reserve" while he lived, Chopin declares that it is not in "expressions wrung from him by the conventional demands of his daily life" that one can find the person behind the actor. "The *real* Edwin Booth gave himself . . . through his art. . . . Through it he was great, he was individual" (695–96). Chopin would almost certainly have liked for the same thing to be said about "the real Kate Chopin."

Another Chopin review, "Emile Zola's 'Lourdes,'" appeared in the 17 November 1894 issue of *St. Louis Life*. Again, she finds fault with the work under discussion, saying that Zola never for a moment lets us forget "the disagreeable fact that his design is to instruct us." She also remarks that "truth rests upon a shifting basis and is apt to be kaleidoscopic"(697). Thus she clearly believes that fiction should not try to instruct or reform; and she does not claim that she, any more than Zola, always sees all of the "truth." But she finds life from whatever perspective interesting; and whatever the writer's point of view, it can contribute to the reader's total view of "truth."

"Confidences." An unpublished early draft, written in September 1896, of an essay discussing her own work, "Confidences" begins with Chopin's remembering that she once vowed never to "be confidential except for the purpose of misleading." But in Emersonian tones she adds that "consistency is a pompous and wearisome burden to bear" (700), and so she breaks that vow.

She discusses first the effect that her discovery of Maupassant had had upon her eight years earlier, about a year before she herself began writing: "I had been . . . groping around; looking for something big, satisfying, convincing, and finding nothing but—myself; a something neither big nor satisfying but wholly convincing. . . . at this period of my emerging from the vast solitude in which I had been making my own acquaintance, . . . I stumbled upon Maupassant" (700).[17] (By the time a revised version of this essay reached print in the January 1899 *Atlantic Monthly,* Chopin had expunged the description of her search for her own "acquaintance," and nowhere else does she describe so intimately this search for herself.)

Of Maupassant's stories, she declares: "Here was life, not fiction; for where were the plots, the old fashioned mechanism and stage trapping that . . . I had fancied were essential to . . . story making. Here was a man who had escaped from tradition and authority, who had entered into himself and looked out upon life through his own being. . . . he gives us . . .

something valuable for it is genuine and spontaneous" (700–701). Many of the best and worst features in her own fiction Chopin here describes as qualities of Maupassant's work. First, her strength never lies in plotting, although she does sometimes indulge in such "stage trapping" as quaint local-color settings and surprise endings, like that of "Désirée's Baby." Second, her best work grows from her own remarkable ability, like that she attributes to Maupassant, to free herself from "tradition and authority" so that she can enter into herself and look out upon life through her own being, telling what she sees with a direct honesty surpassed by very few authors. And, third, her greatest weakness—her often trite, careless diction—results from her reluctance to revise lest she lose that "genuine and spontaneous" quality, which she so much admires in the French writer.

But Chopin did extensively revise this essay before it came out in a much shorter and less personal version under a new title, "In the Confidence of a Story-Writer." In the later version she says that she cannot work creatively while adhering to a time schedule, that she finds "the intellectual atmosphere of clubs . . . where questions are debated and knowledge disseminated" (704) stifling, and that "taking pains" leads her inevitably to write a dull story. She concludes that "a writer should be content to use his own faculty, whether it be a faculty for taking pains or a faculty for reaching his effects by the most careless methods" (705). In other words, she regards writers much as she does her characters. Some find one way best, some another; most have a part, but only a part, of the "kaleidoscopic" truth.

"As You Like It." The *St. Louis Criterion* published in February and March 1897 a series of six Chopin essays entitled "As You Like It." In the first a persona says: "We never know what illusions are till we have lost them. They belong to youth, and they are poetry and philosophy, and vagabondage, and everything delightful. And they last till men and the world, life and the institutions, come along" (708). This description of illusions brings to mind several of Chopin's better stories: "Miss McEnders," "Désirée's Baby," "Lilacs," "Vagabonds," "The Recovery," "A Vocation and a Voice," and *The Awakening*. In each case the protagonist discovers something about his or her own identity.

In the second of these essays the author reports that she has no "opinions upon books and writers" because "I could do nothing with them; nobody wanted them; they perished of inanition" (709). These words, of course, remind us once again of Chopin's often reiterated hostility to writers who would instruct or moralize.

She declares: "I am not going to advise anyone to read [Alexander Keil-

land's] stories; I would not be guilty of advising anyone to do anything"
(709). But she does describe her own pleasant response to three of Keil-
land's stories and to his volume *Tales of Two Countries*. One of the stories,
"Pharaoh," she says has a "fine psychological touch." In it a countess, lifted
from the mass of "grumbling, hungry-eyed humanity" because her beauty
had attracted a count, rides through a throng of people one day, and "her
heart, her very soul goes out to them . . . with the sympathy of blood. She
wants to be where she belongs, out there with the growling multitude"
(710). The countess, like many Chopin characters, thus discovers that she
needs continuity of self and a place in society where she feels that she belongs. It is small wonder that Chopin admires the story.

The third essay in the series tells of Ruth McEnery Stuart, another local
colorist who set her stories in Louisiana and who had gained more recognition than Chopin at the time. The qualities Chopin admires in Stuart
tell us something about Chopin's conception of the "womanly" woman as
well as something about Stuart. After describing her reluctance to meet a
celebrity—"I had met a few celebrities, and they had never failed to de-
press me"—Chopin says: "But pshaw! . . . I might have known that a
woman possessing so great an abundance of the saving grace—which is
humor—was not going to take herself seriously." Chopin describes Stuart's
personality, voice, and appearance; but then she gets to the part that
counts, the inmost being, the "soul":

there are no sharp edges to this woman's soul, no unsheathed prejudices dwelling
therein wherewith to inflict wound, or prick, or stab upon her fellow-man or
woman.
    Mrs. Stuart, in fact, is a delightful womanly woman. . . . I know she would
not have bored me the whole day long. (712)

Thus does Chopin make plain her own image of a "womanly woman"; how
it differs from Mr. Buddie Bénoîte's in "The Gentleman from New Orleans," who regards his wife's "lack of self assertion . . . as the perfection
of womanliness" (631)!

Essay 4 in the *Criterion* series argues against book-banning, an activity
Chopin believes to be self-defeating at best. First, she says, "It is . . .
robbing youth of its privilege to gather wisdom as the bee gathers honey"
(713). But worse, it also leads young people to read—simply because they
are forbidden—books which are "bad," "dull," and "immoral" because
they are "not true" (714). (Chopin wrote this essay well before her own
hometown library banned *The Awakening*.)

Number 5 in the series ironically describes Chopin herself attempting to put together her memoirs. When she tries to recall the incidents that give to her childhood and youth their aura of pleasant excitement, she can remember nothing that contributes to a heroic concept of herself. So Chopin suggests that if she writes heroic memories, she lacks honesty; yet if she records her true memories, she will only bore her readers. And in either case, she implies that only egotism leads her to think that her own past really interests anyone except herself.

The last *Criterion* essay reviews *Sister Jane* by Joel Chandler Harris, a novel that Chopin says "has come perilously near being ruined by a plot." Further, she declares, "A singular feature of the book is that the real characters in it have absolutely nothing to do with the furtherance of the plot: they are the author's own, and every one of them is a masterpiece of his creative genius" (719). She adds that Harris

has the power to depict character in its outward manifestations, unsurpassed by any American writer of the present day and equalled by few.

Let us hope that he will tell us more of those old-time people . . . of Middle Georgia. We shall not demand a plot; just a record of their plain and simple lives is all we want. (720)

Thus Chopin implies again what she says directly in the earlier essay "In the Confidence of a Story-Writer": an author needs to recognize his or her "own faculty" and to use it without feeling discontent about the audiences he or she cannot reach. In fact, she repeatedly shows that, whether as writers or as persons, people must know and accept themselves; only if they gain at least a modicum of personal satisfaction from their own "faculty" or "place," as the case may be, will they function well.

"Like tearing a flower to pieces." Chopin published her last essay in the *St. Louis Post-Dispatch* on 26 November 1899. In it she answers with light satire such personal questions as "where, when, why, what do you write?" (721). She declares that, with her, "Story-writing . . . is the spontaneous expression of impressions gathered goodness knows where. To seek the source, the impulse of a story is like tearing a flower to pieces for wantonness." Elaborating further on this spontaneity in her own creative processes, she adds: "I am completely at the mercy of unconscious selection. To such an extent is this true, that what is called the polishing up process has always proved disastrous to my work, and I avoid it, preferring the integrity of crudities to artificialities" (722).

In this essay, published seven months after *The Awakening* had appeared, she says that her friends and acquaintances often ask her where they can find her "latest book." With unusual acidity she quotes such a conversation:

> I always try to be polite. "My latest book? Why you will find it, no doubt, at the book-seller's or the libraries."
> "The libraries! Oh, no they don't keep it." She hadn't thought of the bookseller's. It's real hard to think of everything! (722)

This bit of sarcasm, rare in Chopin's writing, bares the bitter hurt she felt about the novel's reception.

The same feeling probably lies behind her description of "the questions which some newspaper editors will put to a defenseless woman under the guise of flattery." Chopin observes that some editors attempt to draw a woman out by asking about her children: "A woman's reluctance to speak of her children has not yet been chronicled." But she adds that her own offspring would be "simply wild if I dragged them into this." She continues describing the impudence of editors: "'Do you smoke cigarettes?' is a question which I consider impertinent. . . . Suppose I do smoke cigarettes? Am I going to tell it out in meeting? Suppose I don't smoke cigarettes. Am I going to admit such a reflection upon my artistic integrity, and thereby bring upon myself the contempt of the guild?"(723). In this last essay Chopin seems to be saying about herself much the same thing she said about Edwin Booth, that the reader who wishes to know the "real" Kate Chopin must seek her through her art.

And then she adds a last sentence that helps to restore her usual objective tone: "In answering questions . . . the victim cannot take herself too seriously" (723). Thus Chopin's sense of humor and her objective perspective clearly survive; her own sense of continuity remains intact.

Chapter Seven
At Fault

Chopin began writing *At Fault* in 1889 and published it herself in 1890 after only one publisher had rejected it.[1] Since she had written only the poem "If It Might Be" and the story "Wiser than a God" before this novel, it naturally suffers from her lack of writing experience. But, as Robert Arner points out, "the early work of any author assumes significance . . . as a point of departure from which to chart future growth and development."[2] Further, Chopin's first novel, although lacking unity of effect, features a veritable gallery of interesting characters, several of whom foreshadow later, more complex ones. The female characters, for example, display most of the different possible roles into which Chopin envisions women moving as they become less secure in the traditional view that "the woman's place is in the home." And, because Chopin had not yet learned to mute her tones and to draw fully developed, complex characters, the reader can by studying these earliest women better understand Chopin's later ones.

The Plots

The main plot of *At Fault* presents Thérèse Lafirme, a thirty-five-year-old Creole widow who successfully manages Place-du-Bois, the Louisiana plantation she inherited from her husband. David Hosmer arrives from St. Louis to establish a saw mill adjacent to her property. They fall in love; but when Thérèse learns that David has been divorced, she sends him back to St. Louis to remarry Fanny, the alcoholic ex-wife, for whom he feels only pity and contempt. Nevertheless, in accord with Thérèse's wishes he again marries Fanny and brings her to Place-du-Bois to live. Of course, she bribes, begs, and steals to get the alcohol her body demands; and matters move from bad to worse for all concerned until the day when her addiction causes her to drown. After a decent interval, Thérèse and David marry and seem well on their way to living happily ever after as the book ends.

A subplot pairs David's sister Melicent and Thérèse's nephew Grégoire Santien in a love affair as tragic as Thérèse and David's proves ultimately happy. Melicent, a flirtatious snob, will not consider marrying a man who speaks broken English, as Grégoire does, but she nevertheless leads him on to disaster. Grégoire, the first of many Creole gentlemen Chopin created, has inherited from his Creole father a high temper and from his French mother indolence. The climax occurs when Grégoire catches an Acadian scoundrel named Joçint setting fire to David's mill and kills the arsonist on the spot without compunction. Melicent, bored by now with Louisiana anyway, leaves for St. Louis without speaking another word to Grégoire. He goes into town, gets drunk, and "raise[s] Cain" (774). Finally he goes to Texas, where he falls victim to a better gunfighter than he. Thereupon, Melicent dons mourning, because by that time St. Louis bores her too. At the end of the novel she is leaving on a trip to the far West, still searching for excitement.

The Women

Besides the major characters of Thérèse, Melicent, and Fanny, a number of minor women weave their way in and out of the novel. Belle Worthington and Lou Dawson, Fanny's "modern" St. Louis friends, exemplify the idle waste of life as lived by some urban women. Mrs. Joseph Duplan, Thérèse's traditionalist neighbor and friend, follows an older pastoral lifestyle. The pseudo-intellectual Mrs. Griesman is dragged in by allusion at the last minute, apparently to illustrate one type of woman not otherwise represented. Even Grégoire's mother, who remains silently in Paris throughout, contributes her bit by revealing one more role or place for women in late nineteenth-century society.

All of these characters differ markedly from most nineteenth-century women in two ways: motherhood rarely occupies their attention and work rarely intrudes upon their time. Thus they resemble some women of the mid-twentieth century who found that, although technology, affluence, and contraception reduced their household drudgery and family size, these same liberators also sometimes brought excessive leisure and a sense of uselessness. These women in *At Fault* often find themselves with neither a satisfactory sense of continuity in their lives nor a role where they feel that they belong and contribute meaningfully to life.

Thérèsa Lafirme, the complete woman.   The opening paragraph of *At Fault* describes the independent position in life of Thérèse Lafirme, the central character:

When Jerome Lafirme died, his neighbors awaited the results of his sudden taking off with indolent watchfulness. It was a matter of unusual interest to them that a plantation of four thousand acres had been left unincumbered to the disposal of a handsome, inconsolable, childless Creole widow of thirty. A *bêtise* of some sort might safely be looked for. But time passing, the anticipated folly failed to reveal itself; and the only wonder was that Thérèse Lafirme so successfully followed the methods of her departed husband. (741)

Thérèse thus demonstrates the same sort of business acumen that Kate Chopin exercised after Oscar died in 1882, similarly leaving his property to the disposal of a handsome and inconsolable, but certainly not childless, widow of thirty-two.

Thérèse combines a preference for the quiet, settled life-style of the past with an astute business sense that recognizes, even if grudgingly, the inevitability of change. Thus she bows to the encroachment of the railroad upon her serene existence, but when its coming forces her to abandon the old plantation home, she rebuilds "many rods away from the river and beyond sight of the mutilated dwelling." And "In building, she avoided the temptations offered by modern architectural innovations, and clung to the simplicity of large rooms and broad verandas: a style whose merits had stood the test of easy-going and comfort-loving generations" (742). Her housing style matches her personal style.

Thérèse's very feminine appearance belies her business acumen. Her body has "a roundness of figure suggesting a future of excessive fullness if not judiciously guarded; and she was fair, with a warm whiteness that a passing thought could deepen into color. The waving blonde hair, gathered in an abundant coil on top of her head, grew away with a pretty sweep from the temples, the low forehead and nape of the white neck that showed above a frill of soft lace. Her eyes were blue, as certain gems are; that deep blue that lights, and glows, and tells things of the soul" (743). Although not preoccupied with her own appearance as are several other women in *At Fault,* Thérèse does dress tastefully. For instance, as she rides out to see old Morico, Joçint's father, one day, "The dark close fitting habit which she wore lent brilliancy to her soft blonde coloring, and there was no mark of years about her face or figure, save the settling of a thoughtful shadow upon the eyes, which joys and sorrows that were past and gone had left there" (754). And on a train another day, she looks "ruefully at the smirched finger tips of her Parisian gloves. This flavor of Paris . . . was plainly a part of the little black velvet toque that rested on her blonde hair. Even the umbrella and one small valise which she had just laid on the seat opposite her, had Paris written plain upon them" (869). Thérèse looks as she acts—the complete woman who knows who she is, what she wants, and where she belongs.

Thérèse's manners and actions, like her appearance, enhance her feminine appeal. Kind, warm, gracious, sincerely interested in others' problems, this woman exercises an almost irresistible charm. She fills much of her time with endearing activities like the visit to old Morico referred to above. And the old man reacts to her kindness as most others in the story do. He is "all trembling with excitement at her visit" (755), and he even looks from his rebellious son Joçint to Thérèse "with feeble expectancy of some good to come from her presence there"(756). Thérèse protects Morico from understanding fully his son's arrogant behavior and listens with sympathy to "the long drawn story of his troubles, cheering him as no one else in the world was able to do" (757). Old Morico clearly sees Thérèse as the complete woman, the embodiment of all things good and true.

Even Fanny responds similarly to Mrs. Lafirme: "Thérèse affected her forcibly. This woman so wholesome, so fair and strong; so un-American as to be not ashamed to show tenderness and sympathy with eye and lip, moved Fanny like a new and pleasing experience" (801). Again, Thérèse's magnetic personality works its magic when she has a dinner party including Mr. and Mrs. Duplan, Mr. and Mrs. Worthington, and Mr. and Mrs. Hosmer—a disparate group if ever one assembled. But "Thérèse with her pretty Creole tact was not long in bringing these seemingly incongruent elements into some degree of harmony" (843), communicating in one way or another the warmth of the interest and concern she feels for each.

This warm interest in the concerns of other people, however, leads Thérèse also to be something of a busybody. As David says, "You are not what my friend Homeyer would call an individualist . . . since you don't grant a man the right to follow the promptings of his character" (746).

She responds, "No, I'm no individualist, if to be one is to permit men to fall into hurtful habits without offering protest against it." And she adds that she wants him to know "the good things of life that cheer and warm, that are always at hand" (746).

Grégoire also describes her penchant for interfering in others' lives. He tells Melicent that "Aunt Thérèse, she'd fallen out with father years ago 'bout the way, she said, he was bringin' us up." And he adds, "Oh, they ain't no betta woman in the worl' then Aunt Thérèse, w'en you do like she wants" (751). Thérèse seems to feel that she knows what will bring the greatest happiness to everyone, and she is determined that each will live accordingly.

The combination of wanting everyone to share her own pleasure in the warm, cheering "good things of life" and thinking she knows best how others can discover those "good things" leads Thérèse to assume sometimes an air of self-righteous conceit. The narrator describes her thus: "True, Thérèse required certain conduct from others, but she was willing to further its accomplishment by personal efforts, even sacrifices—that could leave no doubt of the pure unselfishness of her motive. There was hardly a soul at Place-du-Bois who had not felt the force of her will and yielded to its gentle influence" (754). Any person who thinks she knows all the answers to life's complexities may cause others to suffer, no matter how grand her intentions; and Thérèse certainly feels confident of her own answers.

Her reaction to David's account of his marriage perhaps best reveals this aspect of her character. First, upon learning that he has divorced his wife, she demands that he not mention again his love for her. "'There are some prejudices which a woman can't afford to part with, Mr. Hosmer,' she said a little haughtily, 'even at the price of happiness'" (766). And she specifically points out that she does not base her "prejudice" on religion. She then insists that David tell her all about the matter, promising "I shall not misjudge you in any case" (767). But when he has completed his story, she withers him with these words: "The kindest thing I can say, Mr. Hosmer, is, that I hope you have acted blindly. I hate to believe that the man I care for, would deliberately act the part of a cruel egotist." After rendering this harsh judgment in general terms, Thérèse becomes more specific: "You married a woman of weak character. You furnished her with every means to increase that weakness, and shut her out absolutely from your life and yourself from hers. You left her then as practically without moral support as you have certainly done now, in deserting her. It was the act of a coward" (768–69).

This assessment of the Hosmers' marital problems, essentially accurate though it is, reveals Thérèse's own egotism as well as her self-righteousness. And her egotism leads her to believe that she can, by applying a moralistic formula, prescribe solutions to everyone's problems. Thus the tragedy of David and Fanny's remarriage results from Thérèse's, not David's, acting "the part of a cruel egotist." But even as she accepts changes in the external world when confronted with evidence of their benefits, so Thérèse effects a change within herself. She acknowledges at last that she cannot solve everyone's problems and that only her own egotism has led her to believe she can.

In any event, despite her self-righteous conceit, Thérèse more nearly satisfies her needs for love, place, and autonomy than any other woman in the novel. She can do so, first, because she adjusts to changing conditions even while maintaining the old traditions and values that give dignity and beauty to life and, second, because managing her large plantation provides meaningful occupation for her.

Melicent Hosmer, romantic performer.   David's attractive, flirtatious, romantic, and capricious sister, Melicent, contrasts sharply with Thérèse. Melicent looks like her brother—tall and slender with dark hair, skin, and eyes. But here the resemblance ends. Fifteen years David's junior, Melicent seems even younger than her twenty-four years. Her face is "awake with an eagerness to know and test the novelty and depth of unaccustomed sensation" (748). Always conscious of the picture she presents and always seeking a satisfying role to play, she regards life as a stage and herself as the star performer.

Upon returning to St. Louis after Grégoire kills Joçint, she rents a "charming little flat" and hires a "delightful little old poverty-stricken English woman as keeper of Proprieties, with her irresistible white starched caps" because she enjoys envisioning herself in such surroundings. The narrator seems to describe Melicent's own image of herself, standing in "her small, quaint sitting-room, her back to the fire, and her hands clasped behind her. How handsome was this Melicent! . . . A loose tea-gown clung in long folds about her. A dull colored thing, save for the two broad bands of sapphire plush hanging straight before, from throat to toe" (854). Upon learning of Grégoire's death, she instantly tells the maid to get out "that black camel's hair [gown] that Mrs. Gouche spoiled so last winter" (856). The narrator comments, "For a long time—how long she could not yet determine—she would wrap herself in garb of mourning and move about in sorrowing—giving evasive answer to the curious who questioned her" (857). The image of herself immersed in deep mourning over a mysterious lover appeals to Melicent.

This young woman, conscious always of the impression she makes upon others, knows well how to attract men, as her effect on Grégoire illustrates. As they come home from a stroll in the woods one day, "Grégoire's face was a study. Melicent, who did what she wanted with him, had chosen this afternoon, for some inscrutable reason, to make him happy. He carried her shawl and parasol; she herself bearing a veritable armful of flowers, leaves, red berried sprigs, a tangle of richest color. They had been in the woods and she had bedecked him with garlands and festoons of autumn leaves, till he looked a very Satyr" (803). A few minutes later she demonstrates her flirtatious ways further: "Endeavoring to guard her treasure of flowers from Thérèse, who was without ceremony making a critical selection among them of what pleased her, Melicent slid around the bench, bringing herself close to Grégoire and begging his protection against the Vandalism of his aunt. She looked into his eyes for an instant as though asking him for love instead of so slight a favor" (804). Fanny, who dislikes her sister-in-law intensely, tries to console Grégoire about Melicent's leaving Place-du-Bois: "If she likes a person she goes on like a lunatic over them as long as it lasts; then good-bye John! she'll throw them aside as she would an old dress. . . . And the people she's been engaged to! There ain't a worse flirt in the city of St. Louis; and always some excuse or other to break it off at the last minute" (826–27). So, Melicent uses widely her knowledge of how to attract men, but she lacks genuine feelings for the men with whom she flirts.

Extremely romantic, Melicent likes to envision herself as being in love; but whenever a man tries to get close to her, she rejects him. Melicent appears in a pirogue with Grégoire gliding down a quiet Louisiana stream: "The wildness of the scene caught upon her erratic fancy, speeding it for a quick moment into the realms of romance. She was an Indian maiden of the far past, fleeing and seeking with her dusky lover some wild and solitary retreat on the borders of this lake, which offered them no seeming foot-hold save such as they would hew themselves with axe or tomahawk" (750). When Melicent meets Grégoire, his broken Creole English both attracts and repels her. She at first tolerates him, then likes him, and at last decides she loves him.

But Melicent really loves only a romantic image of love, and in this case she has an explicit understanding with herself that "nothing could come of it." She regards her feeling for Grégoire

as a phase of that relentless fate which in pessimistic moments she was inclined to believe pursued her.

It could not be thought of, that she should marry a man whose eccentricity of speech would certainly not adapt itself to the requirements of polite society.

He had kissed her one day. Whatever there was about the kiss—possibly an over exuberance—it was not to her liking, and she forbade that he ever repeat it, under pain of losing her affection. (773)

When she learns of Grégoire's death, however, she remembers his kiss, "and a little tremor brought the hot color to her cheek." The narrator muses, "Was she in love with Grégoire now that he was dead? Perhaps" (857).

Also headstrong, Melicent obeys no one. Even before she enters the story, her brother assures Thérèse, "Oh, Melicent will look after herself"

(746). In the pirogue one day, Grégoire warns her to put down her veil without explaining that a swarm of mosquitoes is about to attack. But since "it was not her fashion to obey at word of command" (749), she suffers several nasty stings before following his advice. Chopin generally favors independent women, but Melicent refuses to accept responsibility and therefore strikes the reader as more spoiled than independent.

For example, Melicent shows no compunction about depending upon her brother financially. Further, she refuses to "burden herself with the suspicion" that David could be having financial problems, because she finds the idea "distasteful" (770). When David warns her to control her spending, she resents his discussing "the disagreeable subject of Expenses" (854). And the end of the novel finds Melicent appealing to David to finance a "magnificent trip through the West" (875). Although her brother "keeps" her well, perhaps Melicent's dependence upon his largess twists and deforms her independent spirit.

A capricious sort of recurring boredom, accompanied by a constant, restless search for excitement, forms the nucleus of Melicent's personality. This ennui may stem from a clash between her strong innate drive for independence on the one hand and her dependent, useless "place" in life on the other. She accepts David's suggestion that she spend the summer in Louisiana: "Hitherto, having passed her summers North, West, or East as alternating caprice prompted, she was ready at a word to fit her humor to the novelty of a season at the South. She enjoyed in advance the startling effect which her announced intention produced upon her intimate circle at home; thinking that her whim deserved the distinction of eccentricity with which they chose to invest it" (748). And Melicent enjoys her visit in the South as long as it offers new faces, activities, and scenes.

At first she eagerly keeps house for her brother; but when the Negroes prove reluctant to work for a Northerner, the novelty of housekeeping quickly pales. She finds it exciting to redecorate her brother's cottage "with certain bizarre decorations that seemed the promptings of a disordered imagination" (754–55). She responds ecstatically to Thérèse, telling David with her characteristic exaggeration that "that woman is an angel. She's simply the most perfect creature I ever knew" (760). To Fanny's arrival at Place-du-Bois, Melicent responds first with a hysterical refusal even to "see" her sister-in-law, but then with an effusive embrace and greeting of "poor dear Fanny" (798). To Grégoire's love, she responds first with disdain; then she responds in turn with tender sympathy, with playful flirtation, with bored abandon, with loathing, and finally with romantic nostalgia after learning of his death.

When she returns to the city after the tragedy at the mill, she throws herself into arranging the "quaint" apartment already described and resuming her usual social activities. But she becomes bored with the apartment's very "cuteness" and "quaintness" (854) almost before she finishes arranging it. She detests all her associates and is wallowing in misery before she learns of Grégoire's death. As noted above, at that tragic news she dons mourning and yet another new role: "At all events, for the next month, Melicent would not be bored" (857). So Melicent remains incapable of satisfying any of the basic drives for love, place, or autonomy.

Fanny Hosmer, alcoholic. David's first wife, Fanny, plays a far smaller role in the novel than Thérèse and Melicent. When David had met her, ten years before the beginning of the story, "she was a pretty little thing, not more than twenty, all pink and white and merry blue eyes and stylish clothes" (766). She had a magnetic charm that kept her constantly in David's mind; within two weeks after meeting her, he had asked her to marry him. And they had found happiness together for a time.

A sociable sort of person, Fanny enjoyed being with her friends. But unfortunately her friends and her husband did not enjoy the same amusements or each other's company. So as David's business occupied him more and more, Fanny spent more and more time with her friends, and the couple drifted apart. Long before their marriage, David had come to regard himself as "thoroughly the business man" (766), and as time went on he became busier and busier, turning more and more to his business to fulfill his needs for place and autonomy. He provided generously for Fanny's material needs; but she could only turn more and more to her friends in trying to find a niche where she felt that she belonged, that she was loved and needed. She probably found adjusting to David's preoccupation with his business doubly difficult because she had "always felt herself as of little consequence" (798). Thus the couple began drifting apart even before a year had passed. At that time Fanny gave birth to their son, and for a time she seemed to find in motherhood a promising new sense of who she was. But the child died when he was three, and from then on Fanny's road plunged downhill.

Almost everything that readers know about Fanny they learn through David's account, because by the time the story begins Fanny has long since surrendered control of herself to alcohol. So settled is she in her illness that she greets David's return with "peevish resistance to the disturbance of his coming." Reluctant to resume their marriage, she declares, "It'll be the same thing over again: I don't see what's the use, David." But in only an hour or so David changes her mind, because her "strength of determination was not one to hold against Hosmer's will set to a purpose" (778). For a time after arriving in Louisiana, Fanny does not drink, and she moves feebly toward a new concept of herself as David's wife; but David's love for Thérèse obviously precludes his wife's finding much satisfaction in that role. So denied the opportunity to fulfill satisfactorily any of the basic needs in her personality, Fanny inevitably finds a way to resume the substitute satisfaction she has found in alcohol.

Fanny and Melicent despise each other, but they have at least one important thing in common. David Hosmer handsomely "keeps" them both. When the divorce court orders him to pay alimony to Fanny, he doubles the amount. Because of his generosity, neither Fanny nor Melicent needs to do anything except what she chooses to do; thus both have much idle time. Further, his generosity insures that neither will find a place in life where she feels needed, even by herself.

The magnificent Belle Worthington.   Fanny's friend Belle Worthington, the most significant of the minor women in the novel, exhibits an overwhelming grandeur: "In full garb, she presented the figure of a splendid woman; trim and tight in a black silk gown of expensive quality, heavy with jets which . . . jangled from every available point of her person. Not a thread of her yellow hair was misplaced. She shone with cleanliness, and her broad expressionless face and meaningless blue eyes were set to a good-humored readiness for laughter, which would be wholesome if not musical" (780). Weighing about 175 pounds, this magnificent woman spends a great deal of time and effort on her appearance, which one would never describe as understated.

Belle spends her time adorning herself, playing cards, attending matinees, and gossiping. Her very modern apartment has a Nottingham curtain that "screened her effectually from the view of passers-by without hindering her frequent observance of what transpired in the street" (779); so she keeps a close eye on her neighbors' comings and goings. Her interest in other people's affairs at least matches Thérèse's in magnitude, but curiosity alone motivates Belle's.

Loud and brash, Belle speaks always frankly and usually tritely. Seeing David visiting Fanny before the reconciliation, Belle asserts, "I declare, you might knock me down with a feather" (780). Other favorite expressions include "I give you my word," "that's a horse of another color" (783), "Heavens and earth!" (788), and "It would just suit you to a T" (789). In her last letter to David, Melicent tells about encountering Belle in a St. Louis store: "that impertinent Mrs. Belle Worthington! Positively took me by the coat and commenced to gush about dear sister Thérèse. She said, 'I tell you what, my dear—' called me my dear at the highest pitch . . . 'That Mrs. Lafirme's a trump,' she said—'too good for most any man. Hope you won't take offense, but I must say, your brother David's a perfect stick—it's what I always said'" (875). Tact never interferes with Belle's forthright honesty.

Belle believes in "keeping on the safe side" in regard to religion, being "a good Catholic to the necessary extent of hearing a mass on Sundays, abstaining from meat on Fridays and Ember days, and making her 'Easters'" (784).

Her friendship with Fanny and Lou Dawson, her constant chum, had begun eight years before, when all three women, with their respective husbands, were living in the same boardinghouse. Fanny and David moved into a house, where Fanny remained after their divorce; and Belle and Lou eventually moved with their husbands into ultramodern flats across the street from Fanny's house. Belle and Lou, then, have through the years had very little household work to do.

Belle talks about her husband as if he were not present. She ignores him in other ways as well, for instance using his precious books to prop broken furniture and to hold down wet laundry. That gentleman views life rather philosophically:

Mr. Worthington regarded women as being of peculiar and unsuitable conformation to the various conditions of life amid which they are placed; with strong moral proclivities, for the most part subservient to a weak and inadequate mentality.

It was not his office to remodel them; his rôle was simply to endure with patience the vagaries of an order of human beings, who after all, offered an interesting study to a man of speculative habit, apart from their usefulness as propagators of the species. (782)

Mr. Worthington's low expectations of his wife's mentality, his tendency to view her as an interesting but almost useless curiosity, his monetary generosity that frees her from household responsibilities, and his own personal desire to escape human contacts by withdrawing into his world of books—all these attitudes on her husband's part influence Belle's own concept of herself. As she attempts to satisfy her own needs for love, place, and individuality, she must do so within the framework of her husband's ideas about a woman's place in the world.

Although her husband believes the usefulness of women is limited to their role as "propagators of the species," Belle has only one child, a twelve-year-old daughter named Lucilla. Mr. Worthington's aunt, "a nun of some standing in the Sacred Heart Convent" (782), has charge of the child's training and education. Thus Belle seems hardly even to think of herself as a mother, and the maternal role plays almost no part in her life.

Lucilla, however, does reflect her mother's influence. She makes a rather pathetic figure when her family visits Place-du-Bois: "The pale, drooping girl started guiltily at her mother's sharp exclamation, and made an effort to throw back her shoulders. Then she bit her nails nervously, but soon desisted, remembering that that also, as well as yielding to a relaxed tendency of the spinal column, was a forbidden indulgence" (838). The child's compulsion to "count acts" intrigues Aunt Belindy, Thérèse's housekeeper. Lucilla explains, "Why, an act is something you do that you don't want to do—or something you don't want to do, that you do—I mean that you don't do" (841). The old black woman observes sagely: "W'at dat kine o' fool talk dey larns gals up yonda tu Sent Lous? An' huh ma a putty woman; yas, bless me; all dress up fittin' to kill. Don' 'pear like she studyin' 'bout ax" (842). Thus even Aunt Belindy observes that the grandiose Belle's warped adjustment to life is wreaking havoc with her daughter's developing womanhood.

Lou Dawson, femme fatale. Fanny's other St. Louis friend, Lou Dawson, appears only briefly, but she nevertheless illustrates another way a woman may attempt to compensate for feelings of loneliness and uselessness. Most people consider Lou "handsome," but "no one could have told why, for her beauty was a thing which could not be defined. She was tall and thin, with hair, eyes, and complexion of a brownish neutral tint, and bore in face and figure, a stamp of defiance which probably accounted for a certain eccentricity in eschewing hair dyes and cosmetics" (779–80). Thus even Lou's appearance publishes her strong drive toward personal freedom.

Her husband, a traveling salesman, exhibits a hearty, genial, sporting attitude toward life. He and Lou get along together beautifully; he regards her as "up to the mark and game every time; feminine characteristics which he apparently held in high esteem" (783). When he comes home every two weeks or so, they have a prolonged party until time for him to leave again. Like the other husbands in Chopin's first novel, he provides funds generously, and his wife has no necessity to do anything except kill time until he comes home for another brief visit.

Lou knows well how to appeal to men, and she is attracted by them too. One day she and Belle attend a matinee using tickets given them by two married men whom they know slightly. Afterward, Belle is "resolute in her refusal to make one of a proposed supper party." But "A quiet sideward look from Mrs. Dawson, told Mr. Rodney as plainly as words, that . . . he might count upon her for a *tête-à-tête*" (784). Thus the reader is prepared to learn that Mr. Dawson has shot Mr. Rodney, news which eventually comes in Melicent's final letter to David.

Lou Dawson and her husband really contribute nothing to either the main or the subsidiary plot. They add to the novel only another example of marriage gone wrong. And the only discernible problem with the marriage, Lou's unfaithfulness, results from her idleness and loneliness. Having love and a place of importance to someone only a few days a month does not satisfy a person's basic needs, especially for a woman with a strong innate sexual drive and a similar urge toward autonomy.

Other women: traditional, neglectful, intellectual. Mrs. Joseph Duplan also appears among the guests at the dinner party Thérèse gives while the Worthingtons are visiting Place-du-Bois. Mrs. Duplan heightens Belle's crass modernity by contrast: "This was a delicate refined little woman, somewhat old-fashioned and stranded in her incapability to keep pace with the modern conduct of life; but giving her views with a pretty self-confidence, that showed her a ruler in her peculiar realm." Belle's "splendid" figure, "so blonde" hair, "so brightly" colored and "scintillating" gown rather overshadow the figure of Mrs. Duplan, dressed in "black silk of a by-gone fashion" (843).

Mrs. Duplan and Belle, however, share the distinction of being the only mothers who actually appear among the many women of the novel; the Duplans also have only one child, a daughter named Ninette. Although about the same age, Lucilla and Ninette differ dramatically. The Duplan child exhibits grace, beauty, style, love for fun, and a bit of rebellious spirit. Perhaps both Lucilla and Ninette are trying to establish their own individuality by rejecting their mothers' approaches to life. At any rate, the appearances, manners, and interests of the daughters contrast as sharply as those of their mothers. And Mrs. Duplan's old-fashioned, feminine nonentity clearly produces effects on both mother and daughter that are preferable to those produced by Belle's aggressively modern style.

Two more women, Madame Santien and Mrs. Griesmann, are introduced into the novel but only as they are perceived by other characters. Of Madame Santien, his mother, Grégoire says that she "never could stan' this country" (751) and therefore had fled to France the moment her husband died, leaving her three sons behind to manage the plantation. After Grégoire's death, Thérèse writes to his mother, "living now her lazy life in Paris, with eyes closed to the duties that lay before her and heart choked up with an egotism that withered even the mother instincts. It was very difficult to withhold the reproach which she felt inclined to deal her, hard to refrain from upbraiding a selfishness which for a life-time had appeared to Thérèse as criminal" (853). Thus the narrator editorializes about Madame Santien's neglect of maternal responsibility. Clearly, a woman's place as mother outranks her right to independence, important though that right is, in the hierarchy of values in *At Fault*.

Melicent's final letter to David describes Mrs. Griesmann, another mother and "one of those highly gifted women who knows everything" (875). One suspects that the author has Melicent toss this new name into the novel at the last minute not only to give Melicent another blind alley to follow into the future, but also to provide an example of a woman who turns to false intellectualism in her attempt to fill the needs that Fanny has tried to satisfy with alcohol, Belle with ostentation, Lou with men, Mrs. Duplan with tradition, and Melicent with interminable excitement.

Mrs. Griesmann's son impresses Melicent: "He isn't handsome; rather the contrary; but so serene and collected—so intensely bitter—his mother tells me he's a pessimist" (875). This brief description suggests that perhaps Mrs. Griesmann is nudging her son to develop into a twisted personality, not the balanced individual a genuinely knowledgeable mother would be encouraging.

And Melicent's final praise of Mrs. Griesmann points up that lady's insincerity and shallowness: "Mrs. Griesmann thinks I ought to wear glasses during the trip. Says we often require them without knowing it ourselves. . . . I'm trying a pair, and see a great deal better through them than I expected to. Only they don't hold on very well, especially when I laugh" (875). Laughter seems to have little place in a life dominated by Mrs. Griesmann's kind of intellectualism.

Importance of work.   Among all these women, only Thérèse actually finds a way to satisfy all three of the needs Chopin treats throughout her fiction. Thérèse does so because, unlike Belle and Lou, she treasures those traditions and values that add warmth and beauty to life; because, unlike Mrs. Duplan, she accepts the inevitability of change and accommodates herself to it, even when the necessary change must occur within herself; and because, unlike every other woman in the novel, she has meaningful, productive work to do.

Belle and Lou are "ladies of elegant leisure, the conditions of whose lives, and the amiability of whose husbands, had enabled them to develop into finished and professional time-killers" (781). This condition of "elegant leisure" that turns women into "professional time-killers" Chopin regards as a potential tragedy for many modern women who no longer are needed, full-time and lifelong, in the home.

Only one who exercises some control over his or her life can possibly achieve a sense of autonomy. The possibility of exercising such control has opened for most women only recently, historically speaking, and for many women a traumatic loss of "place," of feeling secure in being needed, has accompanied the change. Thérèse during her widowhood clearly enjoys both feeling self-sufficient in managing her large plantation and feeling that she is needed by its many dependents. But love, the third of the basic human needs as Chopin views life, Thérèse sacrifices until she and David at last marry. Then, in accord with prevailing custom, Thérèse suggests that her husband "help with the plantation." But David wisely refuses. "'No, no, Madame Thérèse,' he laughed, 'I'll not rob you of your occupation'" (874). And so Thérèse finds it possible to satisfy her need for love without, like the other women in *At Fault,* sacrificing the fulfillment of one of her other needs, those for a place where she feels that she belongs and for a sense of herself as a discrete individual in control of her own life.

Chapter Eight
The Awakening

At Fault launched Kate Chopin's literary career. *The Awakening,* her other published novel,[1] terminated it. And their thematic similarity makes even more striking the symmetry they thus give to her literary life. In *At Fault* she creates a whole bevy of women who feel restless and displaced in modern society. In *The Awakening* she creates one tragic heroine who refuses to settle for less than a full and satisfying answer to Lear's question: "Who am I?"

That the literary career of a woman known for half a century almost altogether as a short-story writer should have begun and ended with her only novels is ironic, but far more so is the effect *The Awakening* has had upon Chopin's literary development and reputation.[2] Thus, although she reaches her highest artistic achievement in this second published novel, its harsh critical reception by her contemporaries brought her career as a writer to a virtual halt. That after having been received so severely the novel should then have been practically ignored for a half-century seems unjust indeed. And now that *The Awakening* has been "rediscovered," its critics may be adding yet another layer to the ironies associated with its critical reception, as through overenthusiasm they force upon it meanings its author never intended.[3]

Three Tragic Women

Three important female characters—Adèle Ratignolle, Mademoiselle Reisz, and Edna Pontellier—appear in *The Awakening,*[4] but not one achieves her full potential as a human being: Adèle settles more or less happily for a partial existence as "mother-woman"; Mademoiselle Reisz settles more or less miserably for a partial existence as artist; only Edna refuses to settle for less than full development as a person, and her desperate search for fulfillment hurtles toward failure from its inception to its tragic finale. Edna's search encounters most of the contradictory forces Chopin marked throughout her earlier work as operating against women as they seek to fulfill the basic human needs for love, place, and autono-

my—the emotional satisfactions the author believes are requisite to a fully
realized human life.

Edna Pontellier. Almost austere in its simplicity, the plot of *The
Awakening* develops around Edna Pontellier, a twenty-eight-year-old wife
and mother, who during a summer vacation at Grand Isle falls in love with
"another" man, Robert Lebrun. Robert, returning her feeling but being
an "honorable" man, flees to Mexico. Edna and her children return to New
Orleans, where she becomes conscious of the lack of satisfaction provided
by her usual social and domestic relationships. She gives up her "reception"
days, severs her contacts with her husband's business associates, renews an
old interest in painting, pursues the new friendships begun during the
summer, and discontinues sexual relations with her husband. Her husband, Léonce, finding the situation incomprehensible, follows the advice
of his wise old friend Dr. Mandelet to leave Edna alone, and goes to New
York on a business venture of several months' duration. The Pontellier
children, Raoul and Etienne, go to visit Léonce's mother in the country at
Iberville during their father's absence. Edna develops a sexual relationship
with Alcée Arobin (who then begins acting as though he, too, owns her),
and moves into a small house that she can finance independently. Robert,
who has never been far from Edna's thoughts, returns from Mexico. She
declares her love for him and tells him that she gives herself where and
when she wishes. At this point a servant summons Edna to the bedside of
her friend Adéle, who is about to undergo her biennial parturition. Robert
promises to wait; but when Edna returns, he has gone, leaving only a message that says "Good-by—because I love you" (997). Realizing at last that
Robert does not respect her right to govern her own life any more than do
Léonce and Alcée, Edna lies awake all night in the utter solitude of this
knowledge. The next morning she goes to Grand Isle, removes her clothes,
and gives herself in suicide to the "seductive" (893) sea.

Adéle Ratignolle, "mother-woman." Edna's "awakening" progresses simultaneously with Adèle's pregnancy; thus the structure of the
novel is related to the basic, natural rhythm of the human gestation cycle.[5]
Edna's self-discovery begins (well before she falls in love with Robert) when
she experiences, on the first evening of the novel, a feeling so vague that
she does not recognize it: "An indescribable oppression, which seemed to
generate in some unfamiliar part of her consciousness" and which "filled
her whole being with a vague anguish" (886). Likewise at the beginning
of the novel, Adèle's pregnancy is so new that her "'condition' was in no
way apparent" (889). During the ensuing months, the "mother-woman's"
gestation progresses, and so does Edna's search for herself, until finally

Edna's tragic suicide follows almost immediately after Adèle's painful childbirth. Thus, although children play only minor roles in this novel, motherhood dominates the lives of both Adèle and Edna. Chopin sees an absolutely inescapable link—basic, natural, and powerful—between the female identity and motherhood.

Accordingly the "mother-woman," Madame Ratignolle, perhaps comes closer to achieving a satisfactory existence than any other woman in the novel, and she does so by building it entirely upon her maternal role, allowing her family to "possess her, body and soul" (1000). As Seyersted remarks, "The Creole and undoubtedly Catholic Adèle is a striking illustration of the patriarchal ideal of the submissive female who writes her history only through her family."[6]

Adèle's body appears to have been designed to lure men, to incubate babies, and to nurture offspring. But light irony tinges this description of her lush beauty:

There was nothing subtle or hidden about her charms; her beauty was all there, flaming and apparent: the spun-gold hair that comb nor confining pin could restrain; the blue eyes that were like nothing but sapphires; two lips that pouted, that were so red one could only think of cherries or some other delicious crimson fruit in looking at them. . . . One would not have wanted her white neck a mite less full or her beautiful arms more slender. Never were hands more exquisite than hers, and it was a joy to look at them when she threaded her needle. (888)

To Edna, Adèle looks like a "faultless Madonna" (890) or "some sensuous Madonna" (891). The motherly woman is "more careful of her complexion" (894) than Edna, and dresses in "ruffles," "draperies," and "fluttering things" that "suited her rich, luxuriant beauty" (895).

Adèle's marriage is as nearly perfect as her feminine beauty. The idea that her husband, Alphonse, might be jealous causes laughter among all who know them: "The right hand jealous of the left! The heart jealous of the soul!" (890–91). She puts his preferences above her own in all things. She hurries home, not so much because she wishes to be there as because "Monsieur Ratignolle was alone, and he detested above all things to be left alone" (921). When Alphonse talks about politics, city news, or even neighborhood gossip, "His wife was keenly interested in everything he said, laying down her fork the better to listen, chiming in, taking the words out of his mouth." In fact, "The Ratignolles understood each other perfectly. If ever the fusion of two human beings into one has been accomplished on this sphere it was surely in their union" (938). The astute reader may sense that this perfect union results more from the extinction of Adèle's individuality than from the fusion of their two identities. But Alphonse is thoughtful, considerate, kind, and generous; and Adèle seems perfectly happy.

As nearly perfect as she is in her wifehood, however, Adèle reaches her apex of perfection in motherhood. When the novel begins, "Madame Ratignolle had been married seven years. About every two years she had a baby. At that time she had three babies, and was beginning to think of a fourth one" (889). There at Grand Isle, she walks "down the long line of galleries" with her queenly "grace and majesty," and "her little ones ran to meet her. Two of them clung about her white skirts, the third she took from its nurse and with a thousand endearments bore it along in her own fond, encircling arms" (892). This mother's hands never lie still; even while she visits with her friends during the hot, idle summer at Grand Isle, her needle busily prepares protection for her little brood against the winter, "when treacherous drafts came down chimneys and insidious currents of deadly cold found their way through key-holes" (888). Even playing the piano Adèle regards as a maternal duty: "She was keeping up her music on account of the children, she said" (904). In fact, Adèle Ratignolle portrays in every way the perfect "mother-woman":

The mother-women seemed to prevail that summer at Grand Isle. It was easy to know them, fluttering about with extended, protecting wings when any harm, real or imaginary, threatened their precious brood. They were women who idolized their children, worshiped their husbands, and esteemed it a holy privilege to efface themselves as individuals and grow wings as ministering angels.

Many of them were delicious in the rôle; one of them was the embodiment of every womanly grace and charm. (888)

That "embodiment," of course, is Adèle.

Despite the light irony in her description of Adèle's perfect adaptation to her place in life, Chopin does not directly suggest that Adèle is less than happy with the role. On the contrary, this Creole woman seems to be delighted with her life, and certainly her husband and children seem to be happy under her warm, ministering care. Thus one might conclude that Chopin believes the richest life for all concerned results when a woman recognizes that her proper place is strictly limited to the home.

But very subtly the novelist undercuts this interpretation by revealing also through Adèle some of the shortcomings of a person's settling for less than full development as a human being. These shortcomings are por-

trayed as a part of the "mother-woman's" character, but their effects extend
to the lives and characters of the family members whom Adèle dominates
through her self-sacrifices.

The most prominent of these flaws, Adèle's preoccupation with her
"condition," her health, her physical body in general, results inevitably
from the fact that her entire sense of who she is depends upon her maternal
capacity. Therefore, she constantly makes her pregnancy a topic of conversation. Even selecting a bonbon becomes a problem, because she wonders
if it is "too rich; whether it could possibly hurt her." She shocks Edna's
Presbyterian prudery by "relating to old Monsieur Farival the harrowing
story of one of her accouchements, withholding no intimate detail" (889).
She takes her youngest child up in her arms, "though, as everybody well
knew, the doctor had forbidden her to lift so much as a pin!" (892). Adèle
plays the piano for the others because her "condition" prevents her from
dancing. She carries a fan, a bottle of "salts," and a cologne-dampened
handkerchief with her wherever she goes. In short, Madame Ratignolle
permits no one near her to forget for long her condition.

Adèle's lack of aesthetic sensitivity makes apparent another limitation of
her total immersion in her role. Although she "keeps up her music" and
plays the piano "very well, keeping excellent waltz time and infusing an
expression into the strains which was indeed inspiring" (904), Madame
Ratignolle lacks the capacity to distinguish between genuine and pseudo
art. The Ratignolles, in keeping with Adèle's musical accomplishments,
entertain every two weeks with a *"soirée musicale."* Assorted friends perform
on various instruments, and "it was considered a privilege to be invited"
(936). Significantly, Adèle never invites Mademoiselle Reisz, the one genuine musician she knows. Clearly, the social nature of these entertainments
takes precedence over the aesthetic. Indeed, Adèle intensely dislikes Mademoiselle Reisz and fails even to recognize that musician's artistry.

Mademoiselle's playing, on the other hand, moves Edna quite literally
to tears. But when she decides to work seriously at painting, Edna goes to
Adèle for "the words of praise and encouragement that would help her to
put heart into her venture," although she realizes that the "true worth" of
her friend's artistic judgment is nil. Upon examining Edna's clearly inferi-
or sketches, Adèle exclaims effusively: "Your talent is immense, dear!"
(937). Edna, although not herself an artist, can respond intensely to aesthetic stimulation, but this capability does not actively develop until after
her "awakening" begins. When Edna first responds fully to music, "it was
not the first time she had heard an artist at the piano. Perhaps it was the
first time . . . her being was tempered to take an impress of the abiding

truth" (906). And Edna's aesthetic responsiveness continues to deepen in tandem with her unfolding awareness of herself as a discrete individual. Adèle, clinging tenaciously to her limited existence as the perfection of motherhood, keeps the door to this sort of response tightly closed.

The most unpleasant aspect of Adèle's character may also grow out of her failure to accept herself as a person apart from her mother role. Even as she perceives herself as a "mother-woman," she tends to perceive others in stereotyped terms also. For example, after Robert Lebrun dramatically announces that he is going to Mexico, Adèle observes that "those Lebruns are all given to heroics" (925). And when the conversation turns to the way of life Robert will find in Mexico, Adèle also contributes her bit: "Madame Ratignolle hoped that Robert would exercise extreme caution in dealing with the Mexicans, who, she considered, were a treacherous people, unscrupulous and revengeful. She trusted she did them no injustice in thus condemning them as a race. She had known personally but one Mexican, who made and sold excellent tamales, and whom she would have trusted implicitly, so soft-spoken was he. One day he was arrested for stabbing his wife" (924). So, Adèle tends to take the part for the whole in other people, even in whole groups of people, in the same manner that she has taken the "mother-woman" part for the whole of herself.

Adèle's paradoxical reaction to the childbirth experience itself, however, implies the most pathetic effect of a woman's building her entire existence upon the maternal role. She fears and dreads the delivery, but at the same time she approaches it as her moment of glory to be savored to the fullest. Thus her preoccupation with her "condition" becomes excessive long before time for the crucial moment. One day quite early in the story,

Madame Ratignolle folded her sewing, placing thimble, scissors and thread all neatly together in the roll, which she pinned securely. She complained of faintness. Mrs. Pontellier flew for the cologne water and a fan. She bathed Madame Ratignolle's face with cologne, while Robert plied the fan with unnecessary vigor.

The spell was soon over, and Mrs. Pontellier could not help wondering if there were not a little imagination responsible for its origin, for the rose tint had never faded from her friend's face. (892)

But as her "hour of trial" (979) approaches, Adèle suffers genuine, agonizing fear and pain. She sends a servant to summon Edna to her side. When Edna arrives, she finds Monsieur Ratignolle, a druggist, personally preparing medication for his wife. He thanks Madame Pontellier for coming: "her presence would be a comfort to his wife. Madame Ratignolle's sister, who had always been with her at such trying times, had not been able to come up from the plantation, and Adèle had been inconsolable until Mrs. Pontellier so kindly promised to come to her. The nurse had been with them at night for the past week, as she lived a great distance away. And Dr. Mandelet had been coming and going all the afternoon" (993).

Edna finds Adèle in a state of "suffering impatience." "Her face was drawn and pinched, her sweet blue eyes haggard and unnatural. All her beautiful hair had been drawn back and plaited. It lay in a long braid on the sofa pillow, coiled like a golden serpent" (993–94). She is decrying Dr. Mandelet and her husband for their neglect: "'This is too much!' she cried. 'Mandelet ought to be killed! Where is Alphonse? Is it possible I am to be abandoned like this—neglected by every one?'" (994). When Dr. Mandelet arrives, he urges Edna to visit with him in the living room while the labor progresses, but Adèle "would not consent that Edna should leave her for an instant. Between agonizing moments, she chatted a little, and said it took her mind off her sufferings" (994).

Thus does Adèle endure her "hour of trial"—wringing from it every possible ounce of attention. But the intensity of her pain and the reality of her fear dwarf all other considerations, leaving the reader horrified to think that Madame Ratignolle will proudly approach the same state again in a couple of years.

The "mother-woman's" basic insecurity in her limited existence thus becomes pathetically clear. Apparently unable to perceive herself as an individual human being, possessing no sense of herself beyond her role of wife and mother, Adèle exists only in relation to her family, not in relation to herself or the world. A healthy sense of her own worth would surely lead her to object to this biennial suffering; but having tied her entire existence to being the complete "mother-woman," she must continue to conceive and bear children.

Mademoiselle Reisz, artist-woman. Mademoiselle Reisz, the other important subsidiary female character in *The Awakening,* has in abundance the sense of autonomy that Adèle completely lacks. But Reisz's life lacks love as thoroughly as Adèle's abounds in it. Both women have achieved secure, even if not completely satisfying, places in life, Adèle as "mother-woman" and Mademoiselle Reisz as musician.

Reisz's physical apearance contrasts harshly with Adèle's beauty. Mademoiselle "was a homely woman, with a small weazened face and body and eyes that glowed. She had absolutely no taste in dress, and wore a batch of rusty black lace with a bunch of artificial voilets pinned to the side of her hair" (905).

But Mademoiselle Reisz's temperament and personality repulse even
more strongly than her physical appearance: "She was dragging a chair in
and out of her room and at intervals objecting to the crying of a baby,
which a nurse in the adjoining cottage was endeavoring to put to sleep.
She was a disagreeable little woman, no longer young, who had quarreled
with almost every one, owing to a temper which was self-assertive and a
disposition to trample upon the rights of others" (905). Although vaca-
tioning at a seaside resort, she refuses to enter the water; and she declares
that she must eat chocolates to avoid starvation, because of the poor food
served there. She laughs only "maliciously" (930).

When Edna tries to find the pianist's apartment after returning to the
city, she inquires of a grocer in the neighborhood and learns that "He knew
Mademoiselle Reisz a good deal better than he wanted to know her. . . .
In truth, he did not want to know her at all, or anything concerning her—
the most disagreeable and unpopular woman who ever lived in Bienville
Street. He thanked heaven she had left the neighborhood, and was equally
thankful that he did not know where she had gone" (941).

Certainly, no one loves Mademoiselle Reisz. Not one person in the story
ever calls her by her first name, if indeed she has one. Even Edna, although
she seeks out the older woman whenever she feels despondent and although
she is certainly the closest friend the little pianist has, admits that she does
not know whether or not she likes Mademoiselle Reisz.

But even an unattractive, disagreeable artist needs love, and Mademoiselle Reisz seems to be cut off from any possibility of directly fulfilling that
emotional need. She therefore resorts to vicarious satisfaction through Edna's intense emotional reactions. To this end, Mademoiselle Reisz leads
Robert to write to her of his love for Edna, and then she plays stirring love
music while Edna reads the letters in her presence. This pattern of behavior
continues for several months, actually forming the primary link between
the two women.[7]

And Mademoiselle Reisz does create beautiful music. When Edna first
responds deeply to it, after "her being was tempered to take an impress of
the abiding truth," Mademoiselle's playing "sent a keen tremor down Mrs.
Pontellier's spinal column." Although previously accustomed to visualiz-
ing emotions while listening to music, Edna "saw no pictures of solitude,
of hope, of longing, or of despair. But the very passions themselves were
aroused within her soul, swaying it, lashing it, as the waves daily beat
upon her splendid body. She trembled, she was choking, and the tears
blinded her" (906). Only through her music can Mademoiselle Reisz, this
homely, lonely little woman, express herself or communicate with people;
and few can respond with Edna's sensitivity.

The intimate relationship between her artistry and her strong sense of autonomy Mademoiselle Reisz herself makes clear when she tells Edna: "To be an artist includes much; one must possess many gifts—absolute gifts—which have not been acquired by one's own effort. And, moreover, to succeed, the artist must possess the courageous soul." She explains to Edna that the "courageous soul" is "the brave soul. The soul that dares and defies" (946). And another day she tells Edna, "The bird that would soar above the level plain of tradition and prejudice must have strong wings. It is a sad spectacle to see the weaklings bruised, exhausted, fluttering back to earth" (966).

So long as she maintains her strength and her "courageous soul," then, this artist-woman will continue to "soar." But Mademoiselle Reisz's loneliness makes starkly clear that an adequate life cannot be built altogether upon autonomy and art. Although she has a secure sense of her own individuality and autonomy, the place she has established in her personal community lacks love, friendship, or warmth. Most women would probably prefer living Madame Ratignolle's partial existence as "mother-woman" to Mademoiselle Reisz's partial existence as artist-woman.

Edna, however, is truly a tragic heroine.[8] More honest in her self-awareness than Adèle, more dependent upon human relationships than Mademoiselle Reisz, Edna will not settle for living as less than a complete person; but forces beyond her control doom inexorably her search for a full, meaningful, and satisfying individuality.

～ "Awakening" to Life

One critic has called Edna's "awakening" purely sexual;[9] another has called it sexual and "spiritual";[10] still another has described it as a sexual awakening that is "a metaphoric expression of multitudinous awakenings of deeper and still more powerful emotional forces than the relatively uncomplex feeling of aroused passion."[11] Surely, her awakening encompasses more than physical passion since it begins well before her sexual feelings start to stir.

Quietly, Edna's awakening begins merely with a growing awareness of the inadequacy of her existence. She awakens first to a sense of vague dissatisfaction, next to the aesthetic joy of music, and then to the physical pleasure of swimming. Only after this point in the story does she begin to feel a strong sexual attraction toward Robert, and her full sexual awakening does not occur until months later. Edna's sexual awakening, then, follows her awakening to her own individuality, rather than the other way around. In fact, Chopin may well have intended to illustrate that a woman cannot fully respond sexually until she has first achieved some sense of autonomy.

Edna's body. If Edna's sexual nature were the paramount interest in the novel, surely her physical appearance would help to make the point. Thus one might expect that she would look lush and richly feminine, in the manner of Adèle Ratignolle; but in fact, Edna looks quite different. For example, their body types contrast noticeably: "The women were both of goodly height, Madam Ratignolle possessing the more feminine and matronly figure. The charm of Edna Pontellier's physique stole insensibly upon you. The lines of her body were long, clean and symmetrical." Whereas one can hardly overlook Adèle's sensuous beauty, only a viewer "with more feeling and discernment" can recognize "the noble beauty . . . and the graceful severity of poise and movement, which made Edna Pontellier different from the crowd." And whereas Adèle dresses in ruffles and "fluttering things," Edna wears much simpler clothing: "She wore a cool muslin that morning—white, with a waving vertical line of brown running though it; also a white linen collar and the big straw hat which she had taken from the peg outside the door. The hat rested any way on her yellow-brown hair, that waved a little, was heavy, and clung close to her head" (894). Neither does Edna protect her complexion and her hands in the careful manner of her friend. In fact, even after she falls in love with Robert, she seems never to consider using her body as a lure. But Edna is nevertheless an attractive woman, even though she charms differently than Adèle with her voluptuous beauty: "Mrs. Pontellier's eyes were quick and bright; they were a yellowish brown, about the color of her hair. . . . Her eyebrows . . . were thick and almost horizontal, emphasizing the depth of her eyes. She was rather handsome than beautiful. Her face was captivating by reason of a certain frankness of expression and a contradictory subtle play of features" (883). Edna Pontellier thus appears from the beginning to be contemplative, frank, and yet self-contained. And never does she become preoccupied with her physical body.

Edna's marriage. Edna's marriage, six years old when the novel begins, had happened "purely" by "accident." At a time when she imagined herself hopelessly in love with a famous tragedian, she met Léonce:

He fell in love, as men are in the habit of doing, and pressed his suit with an earnestness and an ardor which left nothing to be desired. He pleased her; his absolute devotion flattered her. She fancied there was a sympathy of thought and taste between them, in which fancy she was mistaken. Add to this the violent opposition of her father and her sister Margaret to her marriage with a Catholic, and we need seek no further for the motives which led her to accept Monsieur Pontellier for her husband. (898)

As the daughter of a hypocritical, gambling, toddy-drinking, pious-talking Presbyterian father who had "coerced his own wife into her grave" (954), Edna had little means to fulfill any of her basic needs for love, place, and autonomy before she met Léonce. Therefore, the opportunity to satisfy two of those needs led her into the marriage: "As the devoted wife of a man who worshiped her, she felt she would take her place with a certain dignity in the world of reality" (898). And for six years that third need, the need to be a discrete individual—the unsatisfied need that finally drives her to give up the love and place provided by her marriage—has not noticeably troubled her.

In the beginning Edna accepts her marriage and her husband without question. Like many couples, they often communicate without words. Returning from the beach, Edna reaches out her hand and Léonce wordlessly gives her rings to her. He says he is going to Klein's hotel to play billiards, and Edna asks if he will be back for dinner: "He felt in his vest pocket; there was a ten-dollar bill there. He did not know; perhaps he would return for the early dinner and perhaps he would not. It all depended upon the company which he found over at Klein's and the size of 'the game.' He did not say this, but she understood it, and laughed, nodding good-by to him" (883). Léonce often sends Edna boxes filled with "the finest of fruits, patés, a rare bottle or two, delicious syrups, and bonbons in abundance" when she is away from home. The other ladies at Grand Isle "all declared that Mr. Pontellier was the best husband in the world." And "Mrs. Pontellier was forced to admit that she knew of none better" (887).

Edna's possessive husband.   But Léonce reveals his possessiveness in the first moment of the novel, when he looks at his sunburned wife "as one looks at a valuable piece of personal property which has suffered some damage" (882). When he returns from Klein's hotel late on the night described above, he finds Edna asleep. But being in high spirits after winning at billiards, "he thought it very discouraging that his wife, who was the sole object of his existence, evinced so little interest in things which concerned him, and valued so little his conversation." And so he frightens her into thinking one of the children may be ill in order to rouse her from her deep sleep. Then, "he reproached his wife with her inattention, her habitual neglect of the children. If it was not a mother's place to look after children, whose on earth was it? He himself had his hands full with his brokerage business. . . . He talked in a monotonous, insistent way" (885). Edna finally gets up and goes into the adjoining room to see about the child, whom she finds sound asleep and quite healthy. Léonce finishes smoking his cigar, goes to bed, "and in half a minute he was fast asleep" (886).

Wide awake by now, Edna goes out, sits in the rocker, and cries. "She could not have told why she was crying. Such experiences as the foregoing were not uncommon in her married life. They seemed never before to have weighed much against the abundance of her husband's kindness and a uniform devotion which had come to be tacit and self-understood" (886). But on this particular night, Edna begins to sense the true nature of her husband's regard for her. And so, sitting there alone after midnight, she feels the first stirrings of that force that will eventually drive her into the sea.

Perhaps she feels a bit like Athénaïse in the story of the same name, who does not hate her husband but does "detes' an' despise" (431) being married. Edna does not think of Robert at all, nor does she feel particularly angry toward her husband. Rather, "An indescribable oppression, which seemed to generate in some unfamiliar part of her consciousness, filled her whole being with a vague anguish. It was like a shadow, like a mist passing across her soul's summer day. It was strange and unfamiliar; it was a mood. She did not sit there inwardly upbraiding her husband, lamenting at fate, which had directed her footsteps to the path which they had taken" (886). This vague "oppression" or "mood" will eventually grow into so strong a determination to seize control of her own life that it will cause Edna to give up everything in its pursuit.

Edna's "position in the universe." At this early stage, however, Edna does not realize that she has begun to "awaken," that a "certain light" will soon begin to illuminate her consciousness. When this "light" does begin to dawn, Chopin devotes an entire chapter to a twenty-three line description of Edna's first awareness:

A certain light was beginning to dawn dimly within her,—the light which, showing the way, forbids it.

At that early period it served but to bewilder her. It moved her to dreams, to thoughtfulness, to the shadowy anguish which had overcome her the midnight when she had abandoned herself to tears.

In short, Mrs. Pontellier was beginning to realize her position in the universe as a human being, and to recognize her relations as an individual to the world within and about her. (893)

Thus does the narrator state plainly that Edna is awakening to herself, her individuality, her unique "position in the universe as a human being."

But "her relations as an individual to the world within and about her" clearly form an integral part of that "position in the universe." And the narrator warns that "the beginning of things, of a world especially, is necessarily vague, tangled, chaotic, and exceedingly disturbing. How few of us ever emerge from such beginning! How many souls perish in its tumult!" (893). Yet once the "light" of self-awareness has dawned, Edna would not extinguish it, even if she could. At this point she resembles the beast in "Emancipation," who will never return to captivity, no matter how much he suffers in freedom.

Even as the basic nine-month structure of the novel makes clear that a woman's maternal nature forms an essential part of who she is, so another structure-theme parallel—Edna's developing love for Robert—makes clear that a woman's sexual nature also forms an inseparable part of her whole self. This love begins imperceptibly at about this point in the story and grows until Robert finally rejects her claim to autonomy.

The fusion of individuality, sexuality, and maternity that exists in the fully realized woman, impossible to describe directly, Chopin suggests powerfully through the poetic "ode" to the sea[12] with which she closes this short, crucial chapter:

The voice of the sea is seductive; never ceasing, whispering, clamoring, murmuring, inviting the soul to wander for a spell in abysses of solitude; to lose itself in mazes of inward contemplation.

The voice of the sea speaks to the soul. The touch of the sea is sensuous, enfolding the body in its soft, close embrace. (893)

In these few erotic lines—emphasizing individuality through the references to "solitude," "inward contemplation," and "soul" and built around the powerful image of the sea, the mother of life[13]—Chopin suggests the threefold dimensions of woman-nature. The "ode" is repeated, like a refrain, at the tragic close of the story.

Edna's marriage disintegrates. Once Edna's consciousness of herself as an individual has begun to stir, her relationship with Léonce can do nothing but deteriorate. Although he believes he loves his wife, although he is a kind and generous man, although he seeks and follows the best advice he can get in his marital confusion, Léonce's immersion in the culture that idolizes the "mother-woman" precludes his ever understanding his wife's awakening need for autonomy. If that awakening were primarily sexual, Léonce might have come to understand it; indeed, it might well have improved their marriage. But all the thought patterns of his forty years, his entire way of looking at life, blind him to the fact that a woman may properly have a "position in the universe as a human being" (893) apart from her place as wife and mother.

The Pontelliers' second quarrel of the novel occurs on the night when Mademoiselle Reisz's music first moves Edna to tears. That same night she finally learns to swim, after having attempted all summer to do so. Elated and exhausted, she sits with Robert while waiting for Léonce to come home, and she says: "A thousand emotions have swept through me tonight. I don't comprehend half of them. . . . I wonder if any night on earth will ever again be like this one" (909). While they sit there in silence, Edna begins for the first time to awaken sexually: "No multitude of words could have been more significant than those moments of silence, or more pregnant with the first-felt throbbings of desire" (911). For weeks the "seductive voice of the sea" has been murmuring in the background of Edna's consciousness;[14] for weeks "the shadowy anguish" that followed the earlier quarrel with Léonce has troubled her life, and she has become physically powerful enough to swim alone in the sea for the first time. Robert has been at her side while she experienced all these inner events, and he is at her side on this night when her individuality becomes strong enough to release her sexual nature. Thus Robert, more or less coincidentally, becomes the object of her "first-felt throbbings of desire."

At this moment, Léonce comes home and Robert leaves. Edna remains on the porch, although Léonce calls to her peremptorily to come inside: "She heard him moving about the room; every sound indicating impatience and irritation. Another time she would have gone in at his request. She would, through habit, have yielded to his desire; not with any sense of submission or obedience to his compelling wishes, but unthinkingly, as we walk, move, sit, stand, go through the daily treadmill of the life which has been portioned out to us" (912). But this night, Edna experiences an awareness that she has never known before.

Léonce changes his tone, this time calling her "fondly, with a note of entreaty." But when his wife still refuses to come inside to bed, Léonce becomes angry: "'This is more than folly,' he blurted out. 'I can't permit you to stay out there all night. You must come in the house instantly.'" No longer thinking of Robert at all, Edna settles down to remain indefinitely on the porch: "her will had blazed up, stubborn and resistant. She could not at that moment have done other then denied and resisted. She wondered if her husband had ever spoken to her like that before, and if she had submitted to his command. Of course she had; she remembered that she had. But she could not realize why or how she should have yielded, feeling as she then did" (912). This scene establishes that Edna's psyche, her soul rather than her body, is undergoing the primary awakening. In the presence of Robert, who at this point seems to regard her as a discrete individual, her sexual feelings also begin to stir. But Léonce's possessiveness, by implicitly denying her the right to respond or not at the urging of her body and soul, represses her sexual nature.

Finally, however, Léonce prevails. He silently joins Edna on the porch and lights a cigar, the emblem of his male authority. There he remains, smoking one cigar after another, until at last he subdues his wife's body and spirit, at least for the moment:

Edna began to feel like one who awakens gradually out of a dream, . . . to feel again the realities pressing into her soul. . . . the exuberance which had sustained and exalted her spirit left her helpless and yielding to the conditions which crowded her in. . . .

. . . She tottered up the steps, clutching feebly at the post before passing into the house.

"Are you coming in, Léonce?" she asked. . . .

"Yes, dear," he answered. . . . "Just as soon as I have finished my cigar." (912–13)

The next day, Edna awakens early and spends the day on a nearby island with Robert. In the evening she sits outside alone, again awaiting her husband's return from Klein's hotel and trying to understand what is happening within her: "She could only realize that she herself—her present self—was in some way different from the other self" (921).

The remainder of the summer passes without the Pontelliers quarreling further, although by the time she returns to New Orleans Edna feels consciously her passion for Robert. She sees no conflict between this emotion and her love for Léonce, because "The sentiment which she entertained for Robert in no way resembled that which she felt for her husband, or had ever felt, or ever expected to feel. She had all her life long been accustomed to harbor thoughts and emotions which never voiced themselves. . . . They belonged to her and were her own, and she entertained the conviction that she had a right to them and that they concerned no one but herself" (929). Her rising feelings, however, refuse to remain forever a secret, private, separate part of her being.

Thus one Tuesday a few weeks after her return from Grand Isle, Edna decides not to stay at home and receive guests, Tuesday being the "reception day" she has held during all the six years of her marriage. Léonce expresses confusion and then anger that evening when she tells him that she has been "out" all afternoon:

> "Why, what could have taken you out on Tuesday? What did you have to do?"
> "Nothing. I simply felt like going out, and I went out."
> "Well, I hope you left some suitable excuse," said her husband. . . .
> "No, I left no excuse. I told Joe to say I was out, that was all." (932)

Léonce moves on from lecturing her about this breach to complain about the food, expenses, and Edna's general household management. Finally, he stalks out, declaring "I'm going to get my dinner at the club. Good night" (934).

On earlier occasions, such quarrels have made Edna miserable, causing her to lose her appetite and to study ways better to please her husband. But "that evening Edna finished her dinner alone, with forced deliberation. Her face was flushed and her eyes flamed." After dinner, she goes to her room and looks out the window "upon the deep tangle of the garden below. All the mystery and witchery of the night seemed to have gathered there amid the perfumes and the dusky and tortuous outlines of flowers and foliage. She was seeking herself and finding herself in just such sweet half-darkness which met her moods" (934). That Edna is searching primarily for all of herself—for her own answer to Lear's question, "Who am I?"—could hardly be more directly stated.[15]

But the hopelessness of her situation almost overwhelms her: "the voices were not soothing that came to her from the darkness and the sky above and the stars. They jeered and sounded mournful notes without promise, devoid even of hope. She turned back into the room and began to walk to and fro down its whole length, without stopping, without resting. She carried in her hands a thin handkerchief, which she tore into ribbons, rolled into a ball, and flung from her." Thus Edna's helpless frustration drives her almost to distraction. "Once she stopped, and taking off her wedding ring, flung it upon the carpet. When she saw it lying there, she stamped her heel upon it, striving to crush it. But her small boot heel did not make an indenture, not a mark upon the little glittering circlet" (934). Unable, then, to make even a tiny mark upon the encircling traditions that imprison her, "In a sweeping passion she seized a glass vase from the table and flung it upon the tiles of the hearth. She wanted to destroy something. The crash and clatter were what she wanted to hear" (934). Unable to destroy those powerful imprisoning forces represented by the traditional wedding ring, she destroys the fragile vase instead.

The next morning, "unusually pale and very quiet," she allows her husband to kiss her good-bye: "Edna looked straight before her with a self-absorbed expression upon her face. She felt no interest in anything about her. The street, the children, the fruit vender, the flowers growing there under her eyes, were all part and parcel of an alien world which had suddenly become antagonistic" (935). She decides to try more seriously to develop her ability to paint. Later in the day she has lunch with the Ratignolles, that perfectly fused couple. But "Edna felt depressed rather than soothed after leaving them. The little glimpse of domestic harmony which had been offered her, gave her no regret, no longing. It was not a condition of life which fitted her, and she could see in it but an appalling and hopeless ennui. She was moved by a kind of commiseration for Madame Ratignolle,—a pity for that colorless existence which never uplifted its possessor beyond the region of blind contentment, in which no moment of anguish ever visited her soul." Edna's determination to achieve some measure of autonomy is becoming the dominant force in her life. The narrator says, "She began to do as she liked and to feel as she liked" (938).

The disintegration of the Pontelliers' marriage progresses: "Mr. Pontellier had been a rather courteous husband so long as he met a certain tacit submissiveness in his wife. But her new and unexpected line of conduct completely bewildered him. It shocked him. Then her absolute disregard for her duties as a wife angered him. When Mr. Pontellier became rude, Edna grew insolent. She had resolved never to take another step backward" (939). At about this stage, Léonce seeks the advice of Dr. Mandelet, who recommends leaving Edna alone to get over this passing whim in her own due time. And so Léonce goes off to New York on his business venture.

Before he leaves, Edna tries halfheartedly to explain to Léonce what she is experiencing, but the effort proves hopeless. In fact, sometimes Léonce wonders if Edna is "not growing a little unbalanced mentally. He could see plainly that she was not herself. That is, he could not see that she was becoming herself and daily casting aside that fictitious self which we assume like a garment with which to appear before the world" (939). Thus the narrator again suggests that Edna's awakening is not primarily sexual. As she "becomes herself," she responds more fully to both aesthetic and sexual stimuli. But these reponses are secondary; only by developing as a human being can she come to experience fully the deepest human joys.

Edna, for her part, rarely feels angry or resentful against Léonce personally. She simply decides to do and to think as she pleases. She even cries when he leaves for New York and feels that she will soon grow lonely without him. "But after all, a radiant peace settled upon her when she at last found herself alone" (954). As a matter of fact, "when Edna was at last alone, she breathed a big, genuine sigh of relief. A feeling that was unfamiliar but very delicious came over her. She walked all through the house, from one room to another, as if inspecting it for the first time. . . . And she perambulated around the outside of the house, investigating. . . . The flowers were like new acquaintances; she approached them in a familiar spirit, and made herself at home among them" (955). Even as Edna becomes a different person when she stops belonging to Léonce, so the house seems to take on a different character in the absence of its owner.

Later she decides to move out of Léonce's mansion to a small house she can finance independently, explaining to Mademoiselle Reisz: "It never seemed like mine, anyway—like home" and "The house, the money that provides for it, are not mine" (962). The pianist objects, "Your reason is not yet clear to me," and the narrator adds: "Neither was it quite clear to Edna herself; but it unfolded itself as she sat for a while in silence. Instinct had prompted her to put away her husband's bounty in casting off her allegiance. She did not know how it would be when he returned. . . . but whatever came, she had resolved never again to belong to another than herself" (936). So she realizes that what she wants is not to feel the pride of ownership herself but to escape Léonce's ownership of herself, to leave behind forever her place among his possessions.

But even now she willingly goes along with Léonce's cover story that she has moved so the mansion can be remodeled. Indeed, she even admires the business acumen that motivates the story and the ingenuity that conceives it. Edna continues to admire her husband's many fine qualities—his generosity, kindness, business skill—to the very end, even while realizing that he can never possibly understand or accept her as an individual human being, a person as well as a wife and mother.

Edna's sexual awakening. Stirred by her newly emerging need to be recognized as a person, Edna turns to Robert, who has chosen her as the object of the innocent but flattering attention he each year devotes to one of the married women at his mother's resort. The Creole women he has so honored during previous summers have never taken his attentions seriously; but Edna, enmeshed in forces beyond her comprehension, let alone control, begins to depend upon his understanding presence. For instance, when walking with her husband and the Ratignolles, she hears Robert's voice behind them and wonders why he does not join them: "It was unlike him not to. Of late he had sometimes held away from her for an entire day, redoubling his devotion upon the next and the next, as though to make up for hours that had been lost. She missed him the days when some pretext served to take him away from her, just as one misses the sun on a cloudy day without having thought much about the sun when it was shining" (907). At the end of the day they spend together on the island, following the Pontelliers' quarrel about Edna's not coming to bed at Léonce's command, Robert leaves Edna waiting for her husband to return from Klein's hotel. Edna wonders why: "It did not occur to her to think he might have grown tired of being with her the livelong day. She was not tired, and she felt that he was not. She regretted that he had gone. It was so much more natural to have him stay" (921).

But Edna herself realizes that sexual desire strongly colors her affection for Robert only when he suddenly announces that he is going to Mexico. After he tells her good-bye,

Edna bit her handkerchief convulsively, striving to hold back and to hide, even from herself as she would have hidden from another, the emotion which was troubling—tearing—her. Her eyes were brimming with tears. . . .
For the first time she recognized anew the symptoms of infatuation which she had felt incipiently as a child, as a girl in her earliest teens, and later as a young woman. (926–27)

After he leaves, she feels that his going "had some way taken the brightness, the color, the meaning out of everything. The conditions of her life were in no way changed, but her whole existence was dulled, like a faded garment which seems to be no longer worth wearing" (927). And as her personality emerges during his absence, her passion for him grows apace.

By the time Robert returns from Mexico, Edna has fully emerged from among Léonce's possessions, and she greets him with frank and open joy. He responds, "Mrs. Pontellier, you are cruel" (984). The same Creole, Catholic culture that produced Léonce also shaped Robert, and he understands Edna no better than her husband does. At first Robert avoids her, and then he confesses that he dreams of asking Léonce to set her free to marry him. Her response shocks him deeply:

"You have been a very, very foolish boy, wasting your time dreaming of impossible things when you speak of Mr. Pontellier setting me free! I am no longer one of Mr. Pontellier's possessions to dispose of or not. I give myself where I choose. If

he were to say, 'Here, Robert, take her and be happy; she is yours,' I should laugh
at you both."
    His face grew a little white. "What do you mean?" he asked. (992)

But before Edna can try to explain, a messenger comes to take her to
Adèle.

Upon returning from Adèle's accouchement, Edna finds only a note
from Robert, informing her that he has left—because he loves her. Thus,
Edna learns that her imagination alone has endowed Robert with sympa- -
thetic understanding, that he comprehends no better than Léonce her need
to be recognized as an individual human being, a person as well as a woman. Now she realizes that, inasmuch as he too sees her only as female, not
as a whole person, "the day would come when he, too, and the thought of
him would melt out of her existence, leaving her alone" (999). And finally,
as Edna gives herself at last to the sea, she recalls Robert's last message,
thinking "'Good-by—because I love you.' He did not know; he did not
understand. He would never understand" (1000).

An emphatic surge in Edna's sexual feelings accompanies her developing
autonomy. Unable to satisfy this newly felt sexual need through her husband, whose possessiveness is responsible for its earlier repression, and
equally unable to satisfy it through Robert because he is an honorable man
who flees to Mexico, Edna "gives herself where she chooses"—to Alcée
Arobin. An attractive man, Alcée "possessed a good figure, a pleasing face,
not overburdened with depth of thought or feeling; and his dress was that
of the conventional man of fashion" (957), but Edna recognizes the purely
sexual nature of his attraction: "the effrontery in his eyes repelled the old,
vanishing self in her, yet drew all her awakening sensuousness" (959). Perhaps a paradox of woman's nature makes her incapable of a fully awakened
"sensuousness" (Chopin's euphemism for sexual responsiveness) unless she
has some sense of power over her own responses; but such a fully awakened
"sensuousness" then urges her to surrender the very autonomy that has
made it possible. At any rate, Edna knows well before the event that she
will "give herself," at least her body, to Alcée. But she knows too that
"Alcée Arobin was absolutely nothing to her" (960).

On the evening after Edna learns that Robert is coming home, Alcée
senses that the time has arrived to consummate the seduction. He kisses
her: "It was the first kiss of her life to which her nature had really responded. It was a flaming torch that kindled desire" (967). Then Chopin includes another of the brief, staccato chapters that she uses much like
exclamation points in *The Awakening*. Only fourteen lines long, even short-

er than the chapter that describes Edna's dawning awareness of herself as
an individual human being, this one describes her ambiguous, but honest
and powerful, reactions following her first sexual fulfillment:

> Edna cried a little that night after Arobin left her. It was only one phase of the
> multitudinous emotions which had assailed her. . . . There was her husband's
> reproach looking at her from the external things . . . which he had provided for
> her external existence. There was Robert's reproach making itself felt by a quicker,
> fiercer, more overpowering love, which had awakened within her toward him.
> Above all, there was understanding. She felt as if a mist had been lifted from her
> eyes, enabling her to look upon and comprehend the significance of life, that
> monster made up of beauty and brutality. But among the conflicting sensations
> which assailed her, there was neither shame nor remorse. There was a dull pang of
> regret because it was not the kiss of love which had inflamed her, because it was
> not love which had held this cup of life to her lips. [16] (967)

Thus Edna begins to understand herself as one who possesses "life, that
monster made up of beauty and brutality." Although contradictory emotions boil within her, she accepts them with tremendous honesty, refusing
to feel "shame" or "remorse," yet recognizing her own "brutality" in reaching out for the "beauty" of sexual fulfillment.

Edna's Hopeless Plight

Nothing in the novel makes the hopelessness of Edna's demand to be
recognized as an autonomous individual more tragically apparent than does
Alcée Arobin's behavior after he seduces her. Immediately he assumes a
proprietary air as authoritative as Léonce's. Coming to her home, "he had
found the front door open, and had followed his ring by walking in uncere-
moniously" (968). When she moves out of Léonce's house, Arobin locks
the door behind her and takes custody of the key. He comes uninvited to
her house, where he reads the newspaper and smokes cigars as though he
owns the entire establishment. One evening when she feels depressed and
miserable, she demands that he leave. But "He did not answer, except to
continue to caress her. He did not say good night until she had become
supple to his gentle, seductive entreaties" (976). Even Alcée Arobin, who
"was absolutely nothing to her," believes that he owns Edna.

In her maternal role, as well, Edna encounters resistance to her desire to
become a fully developed human individual. The same culture that deems
woman to belong to man also demands her subordination to his offspring;
Edna's society, therefore, abounds with "mother-women," who "idolized

their children, worshiped their husbands, and esteemed it a holy privilege to efface themselves as individuals" (888).

Since Edna is not one of these, her husband believes that she fails somehow as a mother.[17] During their first quarrel, described above, he reproaches her "habitual neglect of the children" (885). A little later, the narrator comments: "It would have been a difficult matter for Mr. Pontellier to define to his own satisfaction or any one else's wherein his wife failed in her duty toward their children. It was something which he felt rather than perceived" (887). His feeling clearly does not derive from evidence of neglect in the boys' behavior, because they are remarkably self-sufficient, well-adjusted children:

If one of the little Pontellier boys took a tumble whilst at play, he was not apt to rush to his mother's arms for comfort; he would more likely pick himself up, wipe the water out of his eyes and the sand out of his mouth, and go on playing. Tots as they were, they pulled together and stood their ground in childish battles with doubled fists and uplifted voices, which usually prevailed against the other mother-tots. . . .

In short, Mrs. Pontellier was not a mother-woman. The mother-women seemed to prevail that summer at Grand Isle. (887–88)

Thus Chopin carefully, though subtly, establishes that Edna does not neglect her children. She neglects only her mother-woman image.

Edna tries on one occasion to explain to Adéle how she feels about her children and about herself. She says: "I would give up the unessential; I would give my money, I would give my life for my children; but I wouldn't give myself. I can't make it more clear; it's only something which I am beginning to comprehend, which is revealing itself to me" (929). The "something . . . which is revealing itself" does not become completely clear to Edna herself until just before the end, when she does indeed give her life but not her self for her children's sake.

Edna expresses greater warmth toward her children when she feels happy and confident. Thus she treats the little boys with special tenderness after spending a happy day with Robert on a nearby island; but after Robert goes to Mexico, "Edna tapped her foot impatiently, and wondered why the children persisted in playing in the sun when they might be under the trees. She went down and led them out of the sun, scolding the quadroon for not being more attentive" (929). The morning after she has tried to crush her wedding ring with her boot heel, Edna regards the children as "part and parcel of an alien world which had suddenly become antagonist"

(935). But when she learns that Robert is returning from Mexico, she sends "a huge box of bonbons" to the children, along with a "tender message" and "an abundance of kisses" (965).

A few days after moving into her own small house—when "she began to look with her own eyes; to see and to apprehend the deeper undercurrents of life" (978)—she goes to Iberville and spends a beautiful week with the boys, who are completely happy there on the plantation in the possessive care of Léonce's mother. Plainly, they do not need their mother, but they are glad to see her. And,

> How glad she was to see the children! She wept for very pleasure when she felt their little arms clasping her. . . . And what stories they had to tell their mother! About the pigs, the cows, the mules! . . . It was a thousand times more fun to haul real chips for old lame Susie's real fire than to drag painted blocks along the banquette on Esplanade Street! . . .
> . . . She lived with them a whole week long, giving them all of herself, and gathering and filling herself with their young existence. (978)

Edna clearly loves her children, but she does not confuse her own life with theirs. When she leaves them, "She carried away with her the sound of their voices and the touch of their cheeks. . . . But by the time she had regained the city the song no longer echoed in her soul. She was again alone" (978).

When Edna leaves Adèle after the painful childbirth "scene of torture," which Edna has witnessed "with a flaming, outspoken revolt against the ways of Nature," Adèle gasps, "Think of the children, Edna. Oh think of the children" (995). And Edna does "think of the children." She tells Dr. Mandelet vaguely: "I want to be let alone. Nobody has any right—except children, perhaps—and even then, it seems to me—or it did seem—" (995). She returns home and, after discovering that even Robert does not recognize her right to autonomy, she lies awake all night thinking. She knows now who she is:

> She had said over and over to herself: "To-day it is Arobin; to-morrow it will be some one else. . . . it doesn't matter about Léonce Pontellier—but Raoul and Etienne!" She understood now clearly what she had meant long ago when she said to Adèle Ratignolle that she would give up the unessential, but she would never sacrifice herself for her children.
> . . . The children appeared before her like antagonists who had overcome her; who had overpowered and sought to drag her into the soul's slavery for the rest of her days. But she knew a way to elude them. (999)

Thus woman's existence, first and last, intertwines with her maternal nature. Edna's sense of herself as a complete person makes impossible her role of wife and mother as defined by her society; yet she discovers that her role of mother also makes impossible her continuing development as an autonomous individual. So her thoughts as she walks into the sea comment profoundly on the special identity problems Chopin believes that women face: "She thought of Léonce and the children. They were a part of her life. But they need not have thought that they could possess her, body and soul" (1000). Unable to have a full human existence, Edna chooses to have none at all.

Chapter Nine
Conclusions

Every fully realized individual must answer Lear's fundamental question, "Who am I?" And the answer must recognize the dignity and sovereignty of the individual person yet at the same time acknowledge the person's dependence upon relationships with others.

In Chopin's view of the human condition, persons cannot arrive at a satisfactory sense of who they are unless they fulfill or sublimate three basic needs: the need for a place in the social order where they feel that they belong, the need for human love, and the need for a sense of their own individual sovereignty. These three needs Chopin regards as universal human drives, and she portrays all sorts of characters as they attempt to cope with the conflicts inherent among these requirements. Further, since she experienced these needs and the conflicts among them from a woman's point of view, her works naturally reflect this perception.

In her first novel, *At Fault,* almost her first fiction, Chopin portrays a number of characters, all searching in their own ways for a satisfactory sense of who they are. In *Bayou Folk,* her first collection of short stories, Chopin again portrays a variety of people of both sexes and many circumstances in life; and in it she again reveals her interest in the same three related human needs, concentrating especially on the need to belong. *A Night in Acadie,* her second volume of short stories, though also incorporating all three themes, emphasizes the need for love. And the stories in the projected but never published third volume, "A Vocation and a Voice," insist on the importance of achieving a sense of personal autonomy.

Chopin focuses with increasing clarity on the special problems that women face in reconciling their often conflicting needs for place and love on the one hand and individual sovereignty on the other. This focal point begins to emerge in her first story, "Wiser than a God," and becomes sharp in such later stories as "Lilacs" and "The Story of an Hour." "Regret" develops the theme that the fully realized feminine existence cannot be based altogether on personal freedom but must also include maternal love. And "A Respectable Woman" makes clear that sexual desire is an important part of the complete woman. But "Athénaïse," "The Story of an Hour," and many other stories both early and late insist that to live fully a woman must recognize herself to be a discrete and autonomous individual. In "The Storm," Chopin's last important story, which remained unpublished until 1969, the author portrays a woman who simply satisfies her three basic needs without reflecting upon the conflicts among them; but the primary tension of the story derives from the awareness that Calixta's method of fulfilling these needs will almost certainly lead eventually to explosive consequences.

Finally, in *The Awakening,* the novel that both climaxed and foreclosed her brief but brilliant literary career, Kate Chopin puts all her favorite fictional pieces together. She creates a very human, complex, interesting female character—Edna Pontellier; she studies Edna's efforts to satisfy her basic human needs for place, love, and autonomy; she delineates subtly and powerfully the social environment that foredooms Edna's best efforts to satisfy these needs and to answer happily the question "Who am I?"; and she communicates the deep tragedy of this woman who, unable to achieve a full human existence, chooses to be no one. Again, Chopin makes the reader remember King Lear, who laments plaintively, "Nothing can come of nothing."[1]

Chopin lived and wrote approximately three quarters of a century before her time. So long as she confined her work to innocuous local-color stories, her contemporaries accepted her work and indeed praised it. But when she dared to expose the conflicts raging inside of wives and mothers, her contemporaries insulted her personally and, even worse, banned her novel.[2]

Today, however, Chopin's reputation stands high. As discussed in chapter 2, critics are claiming that her work exemplifies whatever school or approach they favor at the moment, whether it be romanticism, realism, naturalism, existentialism, or feminism.

Actually, however, Chopin stands alone, a solitary figure among all those "ism's." Clearly her work reveals the influence of her forebears and contemporaries, including Emerson, Ibsen, Flaubert, Swinburne, and especially Maupassant and Whitman. But her work defies classification as she portrays the dilemma of the modern woman, freed at last from her centures of drudgery but groping uncertainly for a new place in society where she can be accepted as a unique individual and fulfill her needs for both love and autonomy.

Notes and References

Chapter One

1. Christopher Marlowe, *The Tragical History of the Life and Death of Doctor Faustus,* act 1, sc. 1, line 23.
2. William Shakespeare, *The Tragedy of King Lear,* act 1, sc. 4, line 62.
3. Mary Helen Wilson, "Kate Chopin's Family: Fallacies and Facts, Including Kate's True Birthdate," *Kate Chopin Newsletter* 2, no. 3 (1976–77):25–26. The other biographical facts of Kate Chopin's life are from Daniel S. Rankin, *Kate Chopin and her Creole Stories* (Philadelphia, 1932) except as noted.
4. Per Seyersted, *Kate Chopin: A Critical Biography* (Baton Rouge, 1969), 14, quoting William Hyde and Howard L. Conard, *Encyclopedia of the History of St. Louis,* vol. 1 (New York: Southern History Co., 1899), 358.
5. Wilson, "Chopin's Family," 25–31.
6. Seyersted, *Kate Chopin,* 23, quoting William Schuyler, "Kate Chopin," *Writer* 7 (August 1894):116.
7. Emily Toth, "The Misdated Death of Oscar Chopin," *Kate Chopin Newsletter* 1, no. 2 (1975):34, and "The Practical Side of Oscar's Death," *Newletter* 1, no. 3 (1975–76):29.
8. Rankin, *Kate Chopin,* 106, and Kate Chopin's son, Felix Chopin, in *A Kate Chopin Miscellany,* ed. Per Seyersted and Emily Toth (Natchitoches, La., 1979), 166.
9. Seyersted, *Kate Chopin,* 53.
10. Per Seyersted, ed., *The Complete Works of Kate Chopin* (Baton Rouge, 1969) (hereafter cited in the text), includes ninety-five short stories and sketches, one one-act play, twenty poems, thirteen prose essays, and two novels—all of the significant literature Chopin created plus some not so significant. *A Kate Chopin Miscellany* includes every other extant item that she wrote—four fragmentary or incomplete tales, twenty-six poems, a "Common Place Book, 1867–1870," a ten-page diary entitled "Impressions, 1894," and twenty-eight letters.
11. Emily Toth, "Kate Chopin Remembered," *Kate Chopin Newsletter* 1, no. 3 (1975–76):22.
12. Seyersted, *Kate Chopin,* 60.

Chapter Two

1. See Seyersted, *Kate Chopin,* 56–57, 73–74, for brief discussions of critical reception of *Bayou Folk* and *A Night in Acadie,* respectively.
2. See Margaret Culley, ed., *"The Awakening": An Authoritative Text, Con-*

texts, Criticism (New York, 1976), 145–55, for excerpts from contemporary reviews.

3. Rankin, *Kate Chopin,* 172.

4. Cyrille Arnavon, Introduction to *Edna* (Paris: Le Club bibliophile de France, 1953), trans. Bjørn Braaten and Emily Toth, *Miscellany,* ed. Seyersted and Toth, 168–88.

5. Van Wyck Brooks, *The Confident Years: 1885–1915* (New York: Dutton, 1952), 341.

6. Robert Cantwell, "*The Awakening* by Kate Chopin," *Georgia Review* 10 (Winter 1956):489–94.

7. Robert Burton Bush, "Louisiana Prose Fiction: 1870–1900" (Ph.D. diss., State University of Iowa, 1957), 242.

8. Merle T. Jordan, "Kate Chopin: Social Critic" (M.A. thesis, University of Texas at Austin, 1959).

9. Linda Wolfe, "The Work of Kate Chopin: A Critical Evaluation" (M.A. thesis, New York University, 1959).

10. Edmund Wilson, *Patriotic Gore: Studies in the Literature of the American Civil War* (New York: Oxford University Press, 1962), 591.

11. Kenneth Eble, Introduction to *The Awakening* (New York, 1964), xiii.

12. Carlos Baker, "Delineation of Life and Character," in *Literary History of the United States,* ed. Robert E. Spiller et al., 3d ed. rev., 2 vols. (New York: Macmillan, 1963), 1:858–59.

13. Warner Berthoff, *The Ferment of Realism: American Literature, 1884–1919* (New York: Free Press, 1965), 89.

14. Marie Fletcher, "The Southern Woman in the Fiction of Kate Chopin," *Louisiana Historical Quarterly* 8 (Spring 1966):126.

15. George Arms, "Kate Chopin's *The Awakening* in the Perspective of her Literary Career," in *Essays in American Literature in Honor of Jay B. Hubbell,* ed. Clarence Gohdes (Durham, N.C., 1967), 222.

16. Lewis Leary, "Kate Chopin's Other Novel," *The Southern Literary Journal* 1 (Autumn 1968):74.

17. Lewis Leary, Introduction to *"The Awakening" and Other Stories by Kate Chopin* (New York, 1970), viii, xvii.

18. Joan Zlotnick, "A Woman's Will: Kate Chopin on Selfhood, Wifehood, and Motherhood," *Markham Review* 3 (October 1968):5.

19. Ibid., 3.

20. Larzer Ziff, *The American 1890s: Life and Times of a Lost Generation* (New York: Viking Press, 1966), 300–301.

21. Seyersted, *Kate Chopin,* 114.

22. Pamela Gaudé, "Kate Chopin's 'The Storm': A Study of Maupassant's Influence," *Kate Chopin Newsletter* 1, no. 2 (1975):1–6.

23. Lisa Gerrard, "The Romantic Woman in Nineteenth-Century Fiction: A Comparative Study of *Madame Bovary, La Regenta, The Mill on the Floss,* and *The Awakening*" (Ph.D. diss., University of California at Berkeley, 1979).

24. Elizabeth B. House, "*The Awakening:* Chopin's 'Endlessly Rocking Cycle,'" *Ball State University Forum* 20 (Spring 1979):53–58.

25. Lewis Leary, "Kate Chopin and Walt Whitman," *Walt Whitman Review* 16 (December 1970):120–21.

26. Gregory L. Candela, "Walt Whitman and Kate Chopin: A Further Connection," *Walt Whitman Review* 24 (1978):163–65.

27. Bernard J. Koloski, "The Swinburne Lines in *The Awakening,*" *American Literature* 45 (January 1974):608–10.

28. Gladys W. Milliner, "The Tragic Imperative: *The Awakening* and *The Bell Jar,*" *Mary Wollstonecraft Newsletter* 2 (December 1973):21–27.

29. Sharon O'Brien, "The Limits of Passion: Willa Cather's Review of *The Awakening,*" *Women & Literature* 3 (Fall 1975):10–20.

30. Susan Wolstenholme, "Kate Chopin's Sources for 'Mrs. Mobry's Reason,'" *American Literature* 51 (January 1980):540–43.

31. William P. Warnken, "Kate Chopin and Henrik Ibsen: A Study of *The Awakening* and *A Doll's House,*" *Massachusetts Studies in English* 5 (1974–75):43–49.

32. Joyce Ruddel Ladenson, "Paths to Suicide: Rebellion Against Victorian Womanhood in Kate Chopin's *The Awakening,*" *Intellect* 104 (July–August 1975):55.

33. Emily Toth, "That Outward Existence Which Conforms: Kate Chopin and Literary Convention" (Ph. D. diss., Johns Hopkins University, 1975).

34. Emily Toth, "The Independent Woman and 'Free' Love," *Massachusetts Review* 16 (Autumn 1975):647–64.

35. S. K. Oberbeck, "St. Louis Woman," *Newsweek* 75 (23 February 1970):103.

36. Sharon O'Brien, "Sentiment, Local Color, and the New Woman Writer: Kate Chopin and Willa Cather," *Kate Chopin Newsletter* 2, no. 3 (1976–77):16–24.

37. Jules Chametzky, "Our Decentralized Literature," *Jahrbuch für Amerikastudien,* 1972, 56–72, excerpt in *"The Awakening": An Authoritative Text,* ed. Culley, 200–201.

38. Ottavio Mark Casale, "Beyond Sex: The Dark Romanticism of Kate Chopin's *The Awakening,*" *Ball State University Forum* 19 (Winter 1978):76–80.

39. Elmo Howell, "Kate Chopin and the Pull of Faith: A Note on 'Lilacs,'" *Southern Studies* 18 (Spring 1979):108.

40. Donald A. Ringe, "Romantic Imagery in Kate Chopin's *The Awakening,*" *American Literature* 43 (January 1972):580–88.

41. Charles W. Mayer, "Isabel Archer, Edna Pontellier, and the Romantic Self," *Research Studies* 47 (1979):89–97.

42. Anne Goodwyn Jones, *Tomorrow Is Another Day: The Woman Writer in the South, 1859–1936* (Baton Rouge, 1981).

43. House, "*The Awakening,*" 53–54.

44. Susan J. Rosowski, "The Novel of Awakening," *Genre* 12 (1979):313.

45. Otis B. Wheeler, "The Five Awakenings of Edna Pontellier," *Southern Review* 11 (January 1975):128.

46. Lewis P. Simpson, Foreword to "The Art of Kate Chopin: Apprenticeship and Achievement," by Robert Arner, *Louisiana Studies* 14, no. 1 (1975):5–10.

47. Sarah Patricia Hopkins Lattin, "Method and Vision in Kate Chopin's Fiction" (Ph.D. diss., University of Kentucky, 1977), quote from *DAI,* 38:6133A.

48. Emily Toth, "Timely and Timeless: The Treatment of Time in *The Awakening* and *Sister Carrie,*" *Southern Studies* 16 (Fall 1977):271–76.

49. Seyersted, *Kate Chopin,* 192.

50. Nancy Walker, "Feminist or Naturalist: The Social Context of Kate Chopin's *The Awakening,*" *Southern Quarterly* 17, no. 2 (Winter 1979):97.

51. Barbara Culver Van Sittert, "Social Institutions and Biological Determinism in the Fictional World of Kate Chopin" (Ph.D. diss., Arizona State University, 1975).

52. Harry Scott Butler, "Sexuality in the Fiction of Kate Chopin" (Ph.D. diss., Duke University, 1979).

53. Jerome Klinkowitz, *The Practice of Fiction in America: Writers from Hawthorne to the Present* (Ames, 1980), 39–40.

54. Stanley Kaufmann, "The Really Lost Generation," review of *The American 1890s,* by Larzer Ziff, *New Republic* 155 (3 December 1966):22, 37–38.

55. Eleanor B. Wymard, "Kate Chopin: Her Existential Imagination," *Southern Studies* 19 (Winter 1980):376.

Chapter Three

1. The nineteen previously published stories had appeared between 1891 and 1894 in *Vogue, Century, Youth's Companion, New Orleans Times-Democrat, Harper's Young People, Two Tales,* or *St. Louis Life.* See Seyersted, "Bibliography of Kate Chopin's Writings," in *Kate Chopin Miscellany,* 203–11, for dates of writing and publication details for everything Chopin is known to have written. See Seyersted, *Kate Chopin,* for full information concerning her dealings with publishers.

2. See Patricia H. Lattin, "Kate Chopin's Repeating Characters," *Mississippi Quarterly* 33 (1979–80):19–37, for a full discussion of this aspect of Chopin's fiction.

3. Carl E. Bain, Jerome Beaty, and J. Paul Hunter in *Classroom Guide: The Norton Introduction to Literature,* shorter 3d ed. (New York: W. W. Norton, 1982), 38–39, discuss well the "mammy stereotype" aspects of this story.

4. See Robert D. Arner, "Music from a Farther Room: A Study of the Fiction of Kate Chopin" (Ph.D. diss., Pennsylvania State University, 1970), 78–80, for full discussion of Chopin's stereotyped black characters.

5. Rankin describes Offdean as "a real portrait of Oscar in 1870" (*Kate Chopin,* 95).

6. See Peggy Skaggs, "'The Man-Instinct of Possession': A Persistent Theme in Kate Chopin's Stories," *Southern Studies* 14 (1975):277–85, for a discussion of this theme in Chopin's various stories.

7. Seyersted, *Kate Chopin*, 164.

8. Shakespeare, *King Lear*, act 3, sc. 4, line 85.

Chapter Four

1. Orrick Johns, "The 'Cadians," *St. Louis Mirror* (20 July 1911), 5–6.

2. "A Night in Acadie" was written in 1896. Seyersted's dates for all of Chopin's works are accepted in this study. See *Complete Works*, 1003–32, and *Miscellany*, 203–11.

3. Quoted in Seyersted, *Kate Chopin*, 68–69, 209, nn. 61–62. Seyersted says that "A Night in Acadie" is one of only two items Chopin is known to have changed at the suggestion of an editor, the other being "Confidences," an 1896 essay published in *Atlantic Monthly* in 1899.

4. Arner, "Music from a Farther Room," 128.

5. Seyersted, *Kate Chopin*, 142–43; Edmund Wilson, *Patriotic Gore: Studies in the Literature of the American Civil War* (New York: Oxford University Press, 1962), 591; Kenneth Eble, Introduction to *The Awakening*, by Kate Chopin (New York, 1964), xiii. This point is discussed more fully in chapter 7.

Chapter Five

1. Kate Chopin's list of stories to be included in this projected volume has been lost. I follow Rankin's list in my discussion (*Kate Chopin*, 195). Arner makes clear that an earlier list must have existed ("Music from a Farther Room," 178–79), but it too has been lost. See Seyersted, ed., *Complete Works*, 1004–30, for dates and full details about writing and publication of the individual stories.

2. Arner, "Music from a Farther Room," 179.

3. Chopin practiced Roman Catholicism until about 1886; although she never repudiated the faith in which she grew up, she ceased overt participation in it at that time (Rankin, *Kate Chopin*, 106).

4. Ralph Waldo Emerson, "The American Scholar," in *The Complete Works of Ralph Waldo Emerson*, ed. Edward Waldo Emerson, 12 vols. (New York: AMS Press, 1968), 1:81–115.

5. Walt Whitman, "Out of the Cradle Endlessly Rocking," in *Leaves of Grass*, ed. Harold W. Blodgett and Sculley Bradley (New York: W. W. Norton & Co., 1965), 246–53.

6. Seyersted, ed., *Complete Works*, 1017–18; *Kate Chopin*, 210, n. 74; Seyersted and Toth, eds., *Miscellany*, 97–99.

7. Theodore Dreiser, "The Second Choice," in *The Literature of the United States*, ed. Walter Blair and others, 3d ed., 2 vols. (Glenview, Ill.: Scott Foresman, 1953), 2:774–88.

8. Arner, "Music from a Farther Room," 193–94.

9. See Joyce Dyer, "The Restive Brute: The Symbolic Presentation of Repression and Sublimation in Kate Chopin's 'Fedora,'" *Studies in Short Fiction* 18 (Summer 1981):261–65, for further insight into this fascinating character.

10. The discussion of this story is essentially the same as that in Peggy Skaggs, "The Boy's Quest in Kate Chopin's 'A Vocation and a Voice,'" *American Literature* 51 (1979):270–76.

11. Seyersted, *Kate Chopin*, 73.

12. Ibid., 111.

Chapter Six

1. Seyersted, *Kate Chopin*, 31.

2. Susan Wolstenholme, "Kate Chopin's Sources for 'Mrs. Mobry's Reason,'" *American Literature* 51 (January 1980):540–43.

3. Seyersted, *Kate Chopin*, 110.

4. Rankin, *Kate Chopin*, 134.

5. Seyersted, *Kate Chopin*, 97.

6. Ibid., 71.

7. Rankin, *Kate Chopin*, 35.

8. Seyersted, *Kate Chopin*, 72.

9. *Miscellany*, ed. Seyersted and Toth, 92.

10. Arner, "Music from a Farther Room," 252.

11. Seyersted, *Kate Chopin*, 164, says that "The Storm" was written on 18 July 1898; but in *Complete Works*, 1028, and in *Miscellany*, 209, the same writer dates the story 19 July 1898.

12. Seyersted, *Kate Chopin*, 182.

13. Ibid., 180.

14. Seyersted (ibid., 183) discusses "Charlie" as the only story in which Chopin disables a man, and believes that in it Chopin is "subtly hitting back at the males who had labeled her a disgrace and silenced her literary gun because she had represented a woman taking the liberties of a man."

15. Ibid., 172–73.

16. *Miscellany*, ed. Seyersted and Toth, 137.

17. Chopin translated eight of Maupassant's stories into English. See the bibliography of works by Chopin for a list of those stories.

Chapter Seven

1. Seyersted, *Kate Chopin*, 53.

2. Arner, "Music from a Farther Room," 41.

Chapter Eight

1. Chopin wrote another novel, "Young Dr. Gosse, " between 4 May and 27 November 1890, but she destroyed it (Seyersted, *Kate Chopin,* 231).

2. See ibid., 173–81, for summary of the critical reception given *The Awakening* by Chopin's contemporaries; Richard A. Martin, "The Fictive World of Kate Chopin" (Ph.D. diss., Northwestern University, 1971), 185–92, points out the extreme, contrasting positions of both earlier and more recent critics.

3. Martin's central thesis is that modern critics are forcing Chopin's work into literary molds currently fashionable but never intended by the author; he believes, for example, that Chopin meant for readers to censure Edna.

4. This discussion of the three important female characters in the novel is essentially the same as that in Peggy Skaggs, "Three Tragic Figures in Kate Chopin's *The Awakening,*" *Southern Studies: An Interdisciplinary Journal of the South* (formerly *Louisiana Studies*) 13 (1974):345–64.

5. Sylvia Saidlower, "Moral Relativism in American Fiction of the Eighteen Nineties" (Ph.D. diss., New York University, 1970), 440. Seyersted remarks upon the pleasure-pain dichotomy of the conception and the delivery that results (*Kate Chopin,* 146).

6. Seyersted, *Kate Chopin,* 140. Chapter 2 of the present study discusses the similarity between Adèle Ratignolle and such black characters as Oswald in "The Bènitou's Slave" and Wash in "For Marse Chouchoute."

7. Martin believes that Mademoiselle Reisz is a more fully developed Fedora (discussed in chapter 4 of this study) and that her feeling for Edna is homosexual ("Fictive World," 146).

8. See Eble, Introduction to *The Awakening,* xii, for discussion of Edna as a tragic heroine in the classical Greek sense.

9. Kenneth Eble, "A Forgotten Novel: Kate Chopin's *The Awakening,*" *Western Humanities Review* 10 (Summer 1956):263.

10. Seyersted, *Kate Chopin,* 145.

11. Arner, "Music from a Farther Room," 149.

12. The poetic qualities of this passage have been discussed by several critics, probably most fully by John R. May, "Local Color in *The Awakening,*" *Southern Review* 6 (Autumn 1970):1034.

13. Chopin's fondness for Whitman is well documented. See Seyersted, *Kate Chopin,* 151; Robert Burton Bush, "Louisiana Prose Fiction, 1870–1900" (Ph.D. diss., State University of Iowa, 1957), 268; and especially Lewis Leary, ed., Introduction to *"The Awakening" and Other Stories by Kate Chopin* (New York, 1970), xiii.

14. Joan Zlotnick says, "It is the seductive sea (frequently linked with serpentine imagery) which arouses Edna" ("A Woman's Will: Kate Chopin on Selfhood, Wifehood, and Motherhood," *Markham Review* 3 [October 1968]).

15. For a thorough study of the meanings Chopin associates with night, see

Joyce Coyne Dyer, "Night Images in the Work of Kate Chopin," *American Literary Realism, 1870–1910* 14 (Autumn 1981):216–30.

16. Cf. the boy's mental and emotional responses to his first sexual experience in "A Vocation and a Voice," in *Complete Works,* 541.

17. Several Scholars agree with Léonce Pontellier. See Seyersted, *Kate Chopin,* 153–54; George Arms, "Kate Chopin's *The Awakening,*" 220–22; Saidlower, "Moral Relativism," 458.

Chapter Nine

1. Shakespeare, *King Lear,* act 1, sc. 1, line 84.
2. Rankin, *Kate Chopin,* 172–73.

Selected Bibliography

PRIMARY SOURCES

1. Novels

At Fault. St. Louis: Nixon-Jones Printing Co., 1890.

The Awakening. Chicago: Herbert S. Stone & Co., 1899; New York: Duffield & Co., 1906; New York: Capricorn, 1964; Introduction by Kenneth Eble—New York: Garrett Press, 1970; Introduction by Warner Berthoff—*Redbook Magazine* 140 (November 1972):199–221; New York, Avon, 1972; edited by Margaret Culley—New York: W. W. Norton, 1976.

2. Collections of Short Stories

Bayou Folk. Boston: Houghton, Mifflin & Co., 1894; Ridgewood, N.J.: Gregg Press, 1967; New York: Garrett, 1970.

A Night in Acadie. Chicago: Way & Williams, 1897; Chicago: Herbert S. Stone & Co., 1899; New York: Garrett, 1968.

3. Collected Writings

Leary, Lewis, ed. *Kate Chopin: The Awakening and Other Stories.* New York: Holt, Rinehart & Winston, 1970.

Rankin, Daniel S., ed. *Kate Chopin and Her Creole Stories.* Philadelphia: University of Pennsylvania Press, 1932.

Seyersted, Per, ed. *The Complete Works of Kate Chopin.* 2 vols. Baton Rouge: Louisiana State University Press, 1969.

———, ed. *"The Storm" and Other Stories with "The Awakening."* Old Westbury, N.Y.: Feminist Press, 1974.

———, and Toth, Emily, eds. *A Kate Chopin Miscellany.* Natchitoches, La.: Northwestern State University Press, 1979.

Solomon, Barbara, ed. *"The Awakening" and Selected Short Stories of Kate Chopin.* New York: Signet Classic, 1976.

4. Translations

"A Divorce Case." 11 July 1894. Unpublished. Story by Guy de Maupassant.

"Father Amable." 21 April 1898. Unpublished. Story by Maupassant.

"For Sale." 26 October 1896. Unpublished. Story by Maupassant.

"How to Make Manikins." *St. Louis Post-Dispatch.* 5 April 1891. Popular article, probably French.

"It?" *St. Louis Life* 11 (23 February 1895):12–13. Story by Maupassant.
"Mad?" 4 September 1894. Unpublished. Story by Maupassant.
"Monsieur Pierre." *St. Louis Post-Dispatch,* 8 August 1892. Story by Adrien Vely.
"Night." 8 March 1895. Unpublished. Story by Maupassant.
"Revival of Wrestling." *St. Louis Post-Dispatch,* 8 March 1891. Popular article, probably French.
"The Shape of the Head." *St. Louis Post-Dispatch,* 25 January 1891. Popular article, probably French.
"Solitude." *St. Louis Life* 13 (28 December 1895):30. Story by Maupassant.
"Suicide." *St. Louis Republic,* 5 June 1898. Story by Maupassant.

5. Films
The End of August. Screenplay by Anna Thomas and Gregory Nava, based on *The Awakening* by Kate Chopin. Quarter Films, Inc., 1982.
Kate Chopin's "The Story of an Hour." New York: Ishtar, 1982.

SECONDARY SOURCES

1. Bibliographies of works by Chopin
Seyersted, Per. "Appendix." In *Complete Works of Kate Chopin,* 1003–32. For each item in the *Works,* this appendix gives date of composition; first magazine and/or book in which item was published, with date; differences in wording between manuscript and periodical form and/or between the magazine and book versions; and additional information.
————, and Toth, Emily. "Bibliography of Kate Chopin's Writings." In *A Kate Chopin Miscellany,* 203–11. A listing of all novels, stories, poems, essays, and the play by Chopin as well as her diaries, extant letters, inscriptions, statements, pieces of music, and translations. Arranged in order of composition, listings include final title, type of writing, date of composition, date of first appearance in print, and full information about the work's inclusion in collections.

2. Bibliographies
Bonner, Thomas, Jr. "Kate Chopin: An Annotated Bibliography." *Bulletin of Bibliography* 32 (July–September 1975):101–5. Excellent listing, still worth checking.
Eichelberger, Clayton L. *A Guide to Critical Reviews of United States Fiction, 1870–1910.* Metuchen, N.J.: Scarecrow Press, 1971. Lists reviews of Chopin's novels and short story collections (68).
Potter, Richard. "Kate Chopin and Her Critics: An Annotated Checklist." *Missouri Historical Society Bulletin* 26 (July 1970):306–17. Largely superseded, but lists theses and dissertations as well as books, articles, and reviews.

Springer, Marlene, ed. *Edith Wharton and Kate Chopin: A Reference Guide*. Boston: G. K. Hall & Co., 1976. Contains virtually everything important about Chopin's works that was published between 1890 and 1973. Excellent, with useful preface.

Toth, Emily. "Bibliography of Writings on Kate Chopin." In *A Kate Chopin Miscellany*, 212–61. Briefly annotated list of books, dissertations, articles, and selected reviews, arranged by year of publication. Exhaustive coverage before 1969 and very thorough from 1969 through 1977, with five entries for 1978. Accurate and insightful in its comments. Largely supercedes earlier bibliographies, upon which it builds well.

————, ed. *Regionalism and the Female Imagination* (formerly *Kate Chopin Newsletter*), 1975–79. This journal carried many good essays about Chopin and her works as well as regularly including a bibliography of works about Chopin. The last issue (Winter 1979) includes an index to all issues (103–6).

3. Books and Parts of Books

Arms, George. "Kate Chopin's *The Awakening* in the Perspective of her Literary Career." In *Essays in American Literature in Honor of Jay B. Hubbell*, edited by Clarence Gohdes. Durham, N.C.: Duke University Press, 1967. Centers attention on Chopin's use of opposites throughout her works, including her ambiguous attitude toward Edna in *The Awakening;* relates this ambiguity to Chopin's view that truth is never absolute.

Jones, Ann Goodwyn. *Tomorrow Is Another Day: The Woman Writer in the South, 1859–1936*. Baton Rouge: Louisiana State University Press, 1981. Believes that Chopin's subject generally was the central symbol of the South's romantic dream, the Southern lady.

Klinkowitz, Jerome. "Kate Chopin's Awakening to Naturalism." In *The Practice of Fiction in America: Writers From Hawthorne to the Present*. Ames: Iowa State University Press, 1980. Finds many influences of naturalism—importance of heredity and environment, threatening environment that causes animal instincts to emerge, sexual frankness, finding vital life lower on the social scale, presence of an understanding scientist—in *The Awakening*.

Leary, Lewis. "Kate Chopin." In *Southern Writers: A Biographical Dictionary*, edited by Robert Bain, Joseph M. Flora, and Louis D. Rubin, Jr. Baton Rouge: Louisiana State University Press, 1979. General, brief summary of Chopin and her works; says that, although her art is excellent, part of her large following results from other factors in her work.

————. *Southern Excursions: Essays on Mark Twain and Others*, 159–91. Baton Rouge: Louisiana State University Press, 1971. Says most of Chopin's works were foretold in *At Fault* inasmuch as it is a story about love and freedom, restricting love versus genuine love and harmful freedom versus enlivening freedom.

Rankin, Daniel S. *Kate Chopin and her Creole Stories*. Philadelphia: University of

Pennsylvania Press, 1932. Rankin saved Chopin's manuscripts from possible destruction; gathered invaluable biographical material, virtually all that is known; and published some of her hard-to-locate stories. But he denounced the eroticism of *The Awakening* and viewed Chopin as merely a local colorist.

Ridgely, J. V. *Nineteenth-Century Southern Literature.* Lexington: University Press of Kentucky, 1980. Critical evaluation of post–Civil War literary movement in the South, where Chopin was among the group of writers who replaced Sims, Timrod, Hayne, Lanier, and Cooke as representative.

Seyersted, Per. *Kate Chopin: A Critical Biography.* Baton Rouge: Louisiana State University Press, 1969. Careful, scholarly biography, well indexed; essential tool for Chopin scholars. Virtually complete bibliography of Chopin's writings. Compares Chopin's works with those of Dreiser, Norris, Garland, and Crane, finding that *The Awakening* stands well in the comparison. Says Chopin's work illustrates woman's right to be independent whether she wants to be a homemaker or a free spirit.

Skaggs, Merrill Maguire. *The Folk of Southern Fiction.* Athens: University of Georgia Press, 1972. A study of American local-color fiction, tracing the tradition that defines the typical Southerner. Many references to Chopin's works, including several pages on *The Awakening,* which is seen as a study of any society in which one person's rights are automatically less than another's.

4. Articles

Candela, Gregory L. "Walt Whitman and Kate Chopin: A Further Connection." *Walt Whitman Review* 24 (1978):163–65. Points to bird images in *The Awakening* as another link, besides those already pointed to by others, with Whitman's poetry.

Candela, Joseph L., Jr. "The Domestic Orientation of American Novels, 1893–1913." *American Literary Realism, 1870–1910* 13 (Spring 1980):1–18. Studies several novels of the period, including Chopin's *The Awakening;* says that Chopin studied women's rights, viewing them as one aspect of a more universal conflict, that between "freedom and responsibility, individuality and family" (7).

Casale, Ottavio Mark. "Beyond Sex: The Dark Romanticism of Kate Chopin's *The Awakening.*" *Ball State University Forum* 19 (1978):76–80. Relates Edna to Hester Prynne and the central figures in *Moby Dick,* rather than to the optimistic transcendentalism of Whitman, Emerson, and Thoreau. Finds Edna's sea unlike Whitman's but like Melville's sea and Hawthorne's forest.

Dyer, Joyce Coyne. "Night Images in Kate Chopin." *American Literary Realism, 1870–1910* 14 (Autumn 1981):216–30. Sees night as equally important with sea to understanding Edna in *The Awakening.* The night is mysterious and sweet, but also tragic and hopeless; the blackness of the night parallels the depth of Edna's soul. Night images are used to state truths otherwise impossible of utterance.

————. "The Restive Brute: The Symbolic Presentation of Repression and Sublimation in Kate Chopin's 'Fedora.'" *Studies in Short Fiction* 18 (Summer 1981):261–65. Calls "Fedora" one of Chopin's best symbolic explorations of repression and sublimation. Points to much evidence supporting interpretation that Fedora is homosexual but concludes that her feeling for Miss Malthers is actually displacement of her feeling for the brother.

Fox-Genovese, Elizabeth. "Kate Chopin's Awakening." *Southern Studies* 18 (1979):261–90. Believes Edna's problems grow out of intense longing for mother that had its roots in her childhood.

House, Elizabeth B. "*The Awakening:* Chopin's 'Endlessly Rocking' Cycle." *Ball State University Forum* 20 (1979):53–58. Follows up on previous analogies with Whitman's poem, analyzing the eros-birth-death natural cycle found in both works.

Howell, Elmo. "Kate Chopin and the Pull of Faith: A Note on 'Lilacs.'" *Southern Studies* 18 (1979):103–9. Sees parallel between Adrienne's and Edna's conflicts; does not believe Chopin was criticizing traditional marriage as institution that suppressed Edna's individual development or the church as an arbitrary institution that refused its comforts to Adrienne. Both characters are simply individual souls at odds with themselves.

Lattin, Patricia H. "Kate Chopin's Repeating Characters." *Mississippi Quarterly* 33 (1979–80):19–37. Views Chopin's stories as related pieces that go together to make up a fictional world larger and more complex than that created in any one story, and many of the characters as more fully developed because of appearing in several works.

McIlvaine, Robert. "Two Awakenings: Edna Pontellier and Helena Richie." *Regionalism and the Female Imagination* 4 (1979):44–48. Views Margaret Deland's *The Awakening of Helena Richie* as a direct condemnation of Edna's behavior in Chopin's *The Awakening.*

Mayer, Charles W. "Isabel Archer, Edna Pontellier, and the Romantic Self." *Research Studies* 47 (1979):89–97. Finds Isabel Archer, although married to a man much like Edna's husband, more responsible heroine than Edna. Sees Edna as egotistical, willful, perverse—one who surrenders to waves of temperament.

Paulsen, Anne-Lise Strømness. "The Masculine Dilemma in Kate Chopin's *The Awakening.*" *Southern Studies* 19 (1980):381–424. Examines various ways the male characters in *The Awakening* respond to the "dilemma" presented by Edna's refusal to act in accordance with society's expectations.

Rosowski, Susan J. "The Novel of Awakening." *Genre* 12 (1979):313–32. Uses five novels, including Chopin's, to illustrate thesis that the "novel of awakening" typically presents a protagonist who moves toward greater self-knowledge, which in turn emphasizes the disparity between such self-knowledge and the nature of society. The protagonist awakens to the limits imposed by a society that allows her to function only as woman, not as human being.

Skaggs, Peggy. "The Boy's Quest in 'A Vocation and a Voice.'" *American Literature* 51 (1979):270–76. Analyzes parallels between the boy's quest and initiation through sexual experience on the one hand and the awakening of Edna's personhood and sexual nature in *The Awakening* on the other.

Thornton, Lawrence. "*The Awakening:* A Political Romance." *American Literature* 52 (1980):50–66. Sees Creole society as deceptive in seeming to offer women more freedom than it allows them to exercise. Edna, although susceptible to romantic codes, comes to understand that she faces a social dilemma that can be escaped only through suicide.

Toth, Emily. "Kate Chopin and Literary Convention: 'Désirée's Baby.'" *Southern Studies* 20 (1981):201–8. Declares the story is about slavery, environment, and the parallel roles of women and blacks.

Walker, Nancy. "Feminist or Naturalist: The Social Context of Kate Chopin's *The Awakening.*" *Southern Quarterly* 17 (1979):95–103. Regards central conflict to be between two cultures, and Edna's awakening to be of the senses only. Edna's emotions, not society or men, dominate her; her suicide results from a "sensual drift," not an existential act of choice.

Wolstenholme, Susan. "Kate Chopin's Sources for 'Mrs. Mobry's Reason.'" *American Literature* 51 (1980):540–43. Relates Chopin's theme that the sins of the parents are visited upon their children to same theme developed more fully by Henrik Ibsen in *Ghosts* and, especially, Richard Wagner in his *Ring* cycle.

Wymand, Eleanor B. "Kate Chopin: Her Existential Imagination." *Southern Studies* 19 (1980):373–84. Believes Chopin to be concerned largely with the existential theme of personhood; points out that Chopin even used terms like "authentic self" and "becoming," which later would come to be heard as the jargon of existentialism.

Index

Arnavon, Cryille, 5
"As You Like It," 69–71
At Fault, 73–87; characters, 74–87; plot, 73–74; theme, 86–87
"Aunt Lympy's Interference," 60
Awakening, The, 5–11, 88–111; analysis of "awakening," 96–108; women characters as partial beings, 88, 94–96

Baker, Carlos, 6
Bayou Folk, 12–26; dislocations, stories of: "Beyond the Bayou," 15; "Old Aunt Peggy," 14; "Return of Alcibiade, The," 16; "Wizard of Gettysburg, A," 16; emancipation of blacks, stories of: "Bênitou's Slave, The," 16–17; "For Marse Chouchoute," 16; love, stories of: "In and Out of Old Natchitoches," 18–19; "In Sabine," 19; "La Belle Zoraïde," 19–21; "Lady of Bayou St. John, A," 20–21; "Love on the Bon-Dieu," 17–18; "Madame Célestin's Divorce," 21; "No-Account Creole, A," 18; "Visit to Avoyelles, A," 21–22; male possessiveness of women, stories of: "At the 'Cadian Ball," 22–25; "Désirée's Baby," 25–26; self-reliant young girls, stories of: "Gentleman of Bayou Têche," 13; "Loka," 13–14; "Rude Awakening, A," 12; "Very Fine Fiddle, A," 13

Cantwell, Robert, 5
"Charlie," 63–64
Chopin, Kate, critical reception of, 4–11; death as reshaper of identity, 2–4; feminist movement, reaction of, 7–8; identity, search for and threats to, as theme, 1, 26, 39, 43, 52, 100, 111,
112–13; literary criticism of, 66–72; local color in works by, 8, 12; poems, 64–66; romantic themes in work by, 8–9

WORKS:
"As You Like It," 69–71
At Fault, 73–87
"Aunt Lympy's Interference," 60
Awakening, The, 5–11, 88–111
Bayou Folk, 12–26
"Charlie," 63–64
"Confidences," 68–69
"Doctor Chevalier's Lie," 58
"Emancipation: A Life Fable," 54–55
"Gentleman of Bayou Têche," 63
"Going Away of Liza, The," 57
"Harbinger, A," 58
"Madame Martel's Christmas Eve," 59
"Maid of St. Phillippe, The," 57
"Miss Witherwell's Mistake," 56
"Mrs. Mobry's Reason," 56–57
Night in Acadie, A, 27–38
"Pair of Silk Stockings, A," 59
"Point at Issue, A," 56
"Real Edwin Booth, The," 67–68
"Shameful Affair, A," 57–58
"Storm, The," 61–62
"Vagabonds," 58–59
"Vocation and a Voice, A," 39–53
"Western Association of Writers," 66–67
"Wiser than a God," 55–56
"With the Violin," 56

"Confidences," 68–69

"Doctor Chevalier's Lie," 58

"Emancipation," 57

"Gentleman of Bayou Têche," 63
"Going Away of Liza, The," 57

"Harbinger, A," 58

"Madame Martel's Christmas Eve," 59
"Maid of St. Phillippe, The," 57
Maupassant, 10–11
"Miss Witherwell's Mistake," 56
"Mrs. Mobry's Reason," 56–57

Natchitoches Parish, 12
Night in Acadie, A, 27–38; stories with
    children as theme, 27–28: "After the
    Winter," 27; "Lilies, The," 27;
    "Matter of Prejudice, A," 27;
    "Mamouche," 27; "Odalie Misses
    Mass," 27–28; "Polydore," 28;
    "Regret," 28–29; "Ripe Figs," 27;
    stories with love as theme, 27, 29:
    "Cavanelle," 31; "Dead Man's Shoes,"
    31; "Dresden Lady in Dixie, A," 29;
    "Neg Creole," 30; "Ozeme's
    Holiday," 30–31; "Tante Cat'rinette,"
    29–30; stories with romance as
    theme: "Athénaïse," 36–38; "Azélie,"
    35; "At Cheniere Caminada," 34–35;
    "Caline," 32; "Night in Acadie, A,"
    32–33; "Respectable Woman, A,"
    35–36; "Sentimental Soul, A," 33–
    34

"Pair of Silk Stockings, A," 59
"Point at Issue, A," 56

Rankin, Daniel, 4, 5
"Real Edwin Booth, The," 67–68

Seyersted, Per, 4, 6–7, 10
"Shameful Affair, A," 57–58
St. Louis Post-Dispatch, 71–72
St. Louis Criterion, 69–71
"Storm, The," 61–62

"Vagabonds," 58–59
"Vocation and a Voice, A," 39–53;
    autonomy as part of self-identity, 39;
    stories with fickleness of fate and
    people as theme: "Blind Man, The,"
    45–46; "Elizabeth Stock's One
    Story," 46; "Kiss, The," 46; "Ti
    Démon," 46; stories with illusion as
    theme: "Recovery, The," 45; "Two
    Summers and Two Souls," 45;
    "White Eagle, The," 44–45; stories
    with power of sex as theme: "Fedora,"
    46, 47–48; "Godmother, The," 48–
    49; "Mental Suggestion, A," 46;
    "Story of an Hour, The," 52–53;
    "Suzette," 46–47; "Unexpected,
    The," 46; "Vocation and a Voice, A,"
    49–52; stories with religion as theme:
    "Idle Fellow, An," 39, 40; "Lilacs,"
    41–42; "Morning Walk, A," 40;
    "Night Came Slowly, The," 39–40;
    "Scrap and a Sketch, A," 40; "Two
    Portraits," 41; stories with suicide as
    theme: "Egyptian Cigarette, An," 44;
    "Her Letters," 43, 44; "Suzette," 42

Western Association of Writers," 66–67
Whitman, Walt, 11
Wilson, Edmund, 6
"Wiser than a God," 55–56
"With the Violin," 56